570

2-21-63

# Men of Athens

# Men of Athens

## Olivia Coolidge

Illustrated by Milton Johnson

1 9 6 2

HOUGHTON MIFFLIN COMPANY  BOSTON

THE RIVERSIDE PRESS  CAMBRIDGE

Books by Olivia Coolidge

Greek Myths
Legends of the North
The Trojan War
Egyptian Adventures
Cromwell's Head
Roman People
Winston Churchill and the Story of Two World Wars
Caesar's Gallic War
Men of Athens

# Men of Athens

# Introduction

THE GOLDEN AGE of Athens is a period of almost exactly
fifty years which was preceded by twenty years of in-
termittent conflict with Persia and brought to an end
by a thirty-year war and defeat by the Peloponnesians.
This whole space between 500 and 400 B.C. is the century
of Athens. Its flowering of genius produced three of the
world's greatest poets and a sculptor of equal rank, besides two other sculptors who in any other company
would be of the first class. The architects of the Parthenon and Propylaea rank with these. Thucydides,
historian of the Peloponnesian War, is in his own way
the greatest of historians. This is the century of Socrates
and the early manhood of Plato. Of Athenian painting
we have nothing left but her incomparable vases. All
the great frescoes of which the Athenians themselves
thought so highly have perished. Indeed, the richness

and variety of the Athenian accomplishment must be
considered not only from the fragments we have left, but
from the vast amount we know existed. Aeschylus,
Sophocles, and Euripides were not the only successful
tragedians. Aristophanes was not the only comedian.
Other writers, philosophers, teachers, and artists are
known to us only by passing references. Some doubtless
are unknown. Such a wealth of achievement can be
compared to nothing in recorded history, except perhaps
to that of Florence. And while the Florentines made immense contributions to learning and art, it was left to the
Athenians to crown their city by a constitution which is
in itself a monument to human aspiration.

Athenian democracy differs from our own in that rep-
resentative government had little place in it. Every
citizen took part in public affairs directly, whether
farmer or aristocrat, poor fisherman or rich merchant.
The chief advantage of money was that its owner was
able to spend it lavishly for the state. He might train
choruses, put on plays, outfit warships, preside at festivals.
His fellow countrymen rewarded him with praise for
what he did well, but the fact that he expended his
money in the public service was taken for granted. The
poor man, too, did his part and frequently gave his life
to glorify his city; for the exuberance of the Athenians
made them aggressive.

This atmosphere in Athens resulted from a rare
balance bestowed on the city by history and chance.
Democracy was young, and the fine traditions of the old

aristocracy were still respected. Corruption and vulgarity were to come, but for the time being the people followed their noblest statesman out of admiration for the sort of man he was. During the fifty years when the democracy was truly great, it lifted the spirits of the Athenians. Their private houses were small and mean; their lives, compared to ours, were poverty-stricken. But they poured out their blood for the city like water; they made her beautiful in marble and bronze, in paintings, in festivals, and in deathless poetry. Critics said sourly that the Athenians were born never to sit quiet themselves or to leave other people alone. But the Athenians called themselves the school of Greece, by which they meant a model for the world.

Even without a great war, it is somewhat doubtful whether so exalted an age could have lasted long. As it was, Athens fell slowly from power while her noble impulses gave way to bluster and greed. Sheer desperation brought cruelty in its train. The Athenian democracy was dragged down spiritually till her famous men were all at odds with her. Finally Plato, perhaps the greatest Athenian of all, rejected politics out of disgust. Yet even in her degenerate days, Athens was a greater city than those of her enemies. Presently she rose again to be the commercial and intellectual center of her world. The traditions of democracy persisted, but the spirit of the city had changed. There were glorious moments still to come; but for the ages, the Fifth Century still remains the century of Athens.

# Prelude to the Golden Age 500–480 B.C.

## The Struggle with the Persians

# Remember the Athenians

## Persia 499 B.C.

IT WAS in the twenty-second year of the reign of the Great King Darius that the Greek cities on the coast of Asia Minor rose in revolt. Some months thereafter in the course of the following summer, one of the Great King's messengers set out on the royal road to the capital, bearing tidings from Artaphernes, brother of the king, who was his governor in Sardis of Asia Minor and who had jurisdiction over the Greek cities of that coast. The messenger's news was of the utmost gravity, as well he knew; but even had it not been so, he still would have galloped where he could and spared no effort. Nothing ever stayed the king's postriders, neither snow, nor

storm, nor flood. Even the brigands who haunted the uplands let them go by, for the power of the Great King
Darius was feared in the remotest parts of his dominions.

The royal road, which had in part been constructed
and was altogether maintained by the Persian king, ran
northeast from Sardis. This was by no means the short-
est route to the capital at Susa, but the postriders from
the Black Sea and the Hellespont used it too, joining
with it not far before the crossing of the Halys. To the
messenger from Artaphernes the river Halys was as yet
a long way off, but it was noticeable that he sped as
though he had not far to go and did not spare his horse.
This royal road was a good one, and wheeled traffic was
forced to turn out of the way for one who traveled on
the king's business. Every fifteen miles or so Darius had
caused way stations to be set up where his men might
change horses at need; but on this occasion rather than
risk unforeseen delay, Artaphernes's messenger kept his
own trusted mount through several stages. He was making good speed, though he was climbing into the uplands where Phrygia and Lydia came together and
where herdsmen pastured great flocks of sheep, where
little market places took the trade instead of towns, and
where most villages were a huddle around one street.
All day he rode; and as the dusk came on, he reached a
way station where a horse stood bridled and ready. Stiffly
the messenger got down and handed his tablets to the
man who waited for them. Untying his horse, this second messenger vanished into the gathering dark, while

the first one took food from his saddlebag and called for wine.

All night the second man rode, letting his horse pick the way, since there was no moon. In the morning of the second day he handed over the tablets to a third man, who took up the tireless trot down the narrow road cut in rock, scraped in sand, trampled into mud, or a mass of shifting pebbles where the rivers flooded it in the spring season. Thus day and night these tablets continuously traveled down the Great King's road to Susa, bearing him news of the disaster which had lately befallen his city of Sardis.

Early in the morning of the third day, it was the fifth messenger who took the tablets in the ferry over the Halys. There was a guard station here to mark the boundary between the old Lydian kingdom and Cappadocia. Every so often it was well for the Great King to know who moved along his road.

In Cappadocia, the messengers rode in streaming rain from drenching thunderstorms, and one of them came limping into the way station late with a horse which had lost a shoe. But the next man was roused in an instant and made off, though he had but a few hours returned from a farther station.

In Cilicia the river Carmelus ran in flood, and there was no crossing for three hours till it went down. Even then the messenger must have a rope rigged across the stream in case the current should sweep him and his precious burden away as he went over.

On the evening of the sixth day the message from
Sardis crossed the Euphrates very high up, near where
the Armenians started down the swift current to Baby-
lon in round skin boats with a cargo of wine and a donkey to carry the folded boat back home up the bank
with its masters trudging beside it. From the Euphrates
the dry and rolling plain, treeless and scrubby, stretched
many miles through scattered settlements to the head-
waters of the Tigris. East of the Tigris, the messengers
turned due south, keeping the river on their right and
the hills on their left as they passed through Media,
where the men wore long linen robes and where the date
palms took the place of the olive, the vine, and the fig of
Asia Minor. Thus passing through Media, hand to hand
and never stopping, the Great King's letter came into
Persia at last not far from the head of the Red Sea Gulf
and arrived in Susa in the hands of the twenty-fifth man
on the thirteenth day, having traveled with a speed unknown to any other thing which moved on the surface
of the earth.

The twenty-fifth man came to Susa in the morning
before the sun was high; and he spoke to the guardians
of the palace, who let him through. But in the court
within the wall the palace attendant whose business it
was to announce such men informed him that Darius
the king was hunting in the hills near where the evil-
smelling spring of petroleum gushed forth. There was
nothing for it but to ride out after the king, which the
messenger did in some trepidation. In the palace he

need not have come into the terrible presence at all. He shook in his shoes, but he galloped out of Susa, lest anyone report that he had lingered.

Darius the king had ridden back from hunting to where his gorgeous tents were pitched, round which his cooks and stewards and grooms and guards and kennel men in furious bustle were preparing for the feast or else removing from his sight all traces of the hunt, now that it was over. King Darius was a square, heavy man of late middle age with a thick, iron-gray beard and a normal expression of considerable good humor. Even the power of life and death over all men had not given Darius a taste for cruelty. His brother Artaphernes was in no fear of losing his life for negligence at Sardis. Nor was the rivalry between his eldest son and his heir Xerxes, born of Atossa his chief queen, allowed to give rise to the murderous intrigues of other princes. Both young men were with him now, one on each side. Both of them reined in their horses while Darius got slowly and stiffly down, and while the cupbearer held out a goblet of wine cooled with fresh snow.

Darius neither accepted nor rejected this. His businesslike little eyes were on the messenger, who threw himself to the ground and touched his forehead to the earth. Not condescending to turn his head, Darius simply beckoned over his shoulder with one finger. His secretary came darting forward in a flash to question the man.

"Whose letter?"

"From Artaphernes, O King of Kings," said the man, his face to the earth.

Even the secretary was too great a personage to take the tablets. He merely nodded in his turn to a lesser slave, who relieved the messenger of his burden, leaving him free to wriggle himself out of sight as best he could.

"Let him be given meat and drink," Darius said.

"I thank the King of Kings," the poor man stammered.

Darius turned from him, leaving him to discover when he dared raise his eyes a trifle that the audience was over and he could get up and go. Meanwhile, the secretary had broken open the seals of the tablet and was perusing the contents with a look of consternation. It was not that the fate of Sardis troubled him, but that his duty was to read aloud to the Great King. All had fallen back except the two princes and the cupbearer, not yet dismissed. But might not Darius consider even this small audience too public for the hearing of unpleasant news? It was the duty of the secretary to know, and he did not know.

A little frown creased Darius's broad brown forehead. The secretary quivered. Slaves were expendable, even the trained ones. In a voice which trembled slightly he read aloud the formal greetings from Artaphernes to the King of Kings and embarked on the letter.

Darius listened grimly. "If we must needs hear such news in public," said he in a voice of displeasure, "let us at least have our audience in proper earshot." He spoke softly; and it might have been supposed that none but the princes, the cupbearer, and the secretary could hear him. Nevertheless, by some peculiar process through which his lightest expression instantly became law, the king's brothers and cousins and brothers-in-law who had been hunting with him moved into ranks behind him while the choking secretary began once more to read the letter.

Darius listened for a moment, flushing with anger. His great, broad hand clenched into a fist was gripping at the front of his embroidered tunic where it showed beneath his beard; but his passion for exact information betrayed itself notwithstanding.

"It was just the Milesians, then, and these Athenians from Greece with twenty ships . . . about two thousand men. Perhaps six thousand in all, and with a few days' rations for a quick raid inland. They beached their ships near Ephesus, you said?"

"Even so, Great King," the secretary agreed.

Darius considered, bringing his vast and detailed knowledge of his dominions to bear on the gaps in his brother's letter. "They must have struck inland up the valley of the Cayster and round the foothills of the mountain of Tmolus. The banks of the Cayster are settled by Greeks, while in the uplands the shepherd folk would be too frightened to send Sardis warning ahead. Very possibly they did not have much time. These Greeks move rapidly, even on a summer's day and in full armor. I have seen them."

"They came on Sardis in the early dawn and must have marched all night," the secretary ventured.

Darius nodded. "Well, read on . . ."

The Greeks had fallen like a thunderbolt on the city of Sardis at the very moment when the sleepy guards were opening the gates. They had swarmed through them, cut down all who stood in their way, and taken the city. Artaphernes, who had a considerable force of Persians with him, had fled for refuge to the citadel, where he had been safe enough until he could summon his forces, which were scattered in garrisons through the countryside.

Sardis was the chief city of the Lydian people, and it was very wealthy. The river Pactolus, which ran right through the market place, brought gold-dust down from Tmolus. The Lydians, moreoever, were famous as hucksters and traders who always knew how to get on. The Greeks scattered in high excitement through the town, disregarding Artaphernes and his guards; and they started to plunder.

The houses of the Lydians, like those of the Greeks, were little and mean, most people preferring to spend their days in the open air. They were generally wattle and thatch, all crowded together, encumbered by booths or shops. They were dotted everywhere with workrooms where iron and bronze were heated, pottery fired, loaves baked, where hearths and furnaces were alight and in the confusion started to blaze. Pretty soon in the suburbs of the town there had been fires which nobody had leisure to put out, all spreading and running together in a delightful breeze which had fanned the Athenians and the Milesians on their night march.

The people of Sardis came swarming out of their houses like bees and took refuge from the flames in the open market place and on the banks of the Pactolus. As a people the Lydians were by no means warlike men; but they were angry, and every head of a house had weapons and armor which hung somewhere on his wall. Besides, many Persians who had been caught in the town were also among them; and these men were warriors all. What with the crowds, therefore, and the increasing resistance, the fires surrounding them, and the menace of the citadel, the Greeks thought it wiser to draw off while they still could. They withdrew, accordingly, from the burning town without much plunder and started back again the way they had come.

Artaphernes, the Persian, meanwhile had not been idle. He had forces scattered in garrisons through the country, and he had immediately sent out messengers. Not many hours after the Greeks had started homeward, strong reinforcements came pouring in, their pace considerably quickened by the glare of burning Sardis and the smoke of it, which was drifting across the uplands into Phrygia. Artaphernes wasted no time. He set out after the Greeks, who, being disappointed with the way the thing had turned out and rather weary from their exertions, saw no need to hurry. Artaphernes caught them outside the walls of Ephesus, forced them to battle, and slew them in immense numbers. Then the Athenians — those of them that were left, completely disillusioned — took their twenty ships and fled home. Artaphernes imagined that they would not be so eager in the future to send help to the king's rebellious slaves in hope of plunder.

This was all very well for Artaphernes to say, but Sardis lay in ashes notwithstanding. The king refrained from comment and stood brooding. The princes of the Persians looked on one another in silent dismay. All of them knew Sardis, one of the richest cities over which the Persian ruled. From the district of Sardis, Artaphernes sent five hundred silver talents in tribute to the king at Susa yearly.

"The Milesians I know," the Great King said at last. "They are my slaves, and I shall punish them . . . but these Athenians . . ." He turned and stared around upon his kinsmen. "Who are the Athenians?" the Great King demanded.

Once more a silent bustle went on in the background. There was a certain Greek whom the Great King out of policy had brought back with him to Susa and seemed to favor. This man, though ruler by rights of Miletus, was of no rank to hunt with Persians. He must, however, trail after his lord with half a hundred others, not appearing unless sent for, but on the spot if ever wanted. Who fetched him now it would be hard to say, but he prostrated himself in the dust before the king and gave information.

"The Athenians," said he, "are a little Grecian people with a territory of a thousand square miles which is mostly infertile. Their single city has thirty thousand fighting men and their dependents. They claim kinship with the Milesians and some of the others of your slaves, who long ago were colonized from Athens."

"I see," the Great King replied. "Then give me my bow."

They brought it, a mighty bow made of two curved horns, with a quiverful of reed arrows.

The Great King fitted an arrow to his bow and shot it high up into the air, a black streak flying and curving, falling across the path of the sun. "God grant me," cried the king to the distant sky, "to have my revenge." He threw down the bow and took the cup of wine, but as he raised it to his lips another thought came. He said to the cupbearer, "Slave!"

"Great King!" The man fell down at his feet.

"Lest I forget this paltry people, you shall remind me. Three times at every feast when you hand my cup, you shall lean over and say as you give it to me, 'Sire, remember the Athenians!'"

The young Xerxes at the king's right hand, ever eager to assert his rights as the heir, nodded to his brother by the lesser wife and said, "This is a good saying and befits the King of Kings. I, too, when my turn comes, shall remember the Athenians."

Then the elder brother scowled on the heir and muttered sourly, "It is easy to remember. Vengeance is hard."

# The Birth of a Lion

## Athens 495 B.C.

AGARISTE had been in labor six hours, and it was nearly morning when the girl slave came down with the child wrapped in a cloth to lay it on the earthen floor at the feet of Xanthippos.

He looked it over, holding the smoking lamp with care lest the hot oil fall on the child. It was a boy and a fine one in all respects well formed, except . . . "The head!" he said sharply to the girl. "What says the midwife?"

It was a strange-looking head, the crown unusually

high and almost pointed. The peculiarity was hardly great enough to be called a malformation, but in such a very young child it was an oddity.

"She says it will change, master." The girl was alarmed. "It was a difficult labor, but he is a healthy child."

Xanthippos smiled in relief. Apart from this one little blemish, the child was as beautiful a one as a man could desire — and a son. Of course he would rear it, and not out of pity either, but out of pride. He set the lamp down carefully in its niche in the wall and stooped to take the infant up. "I do acknowledge him, and he shall be my son. Take him, bathe and swaddle him, and put him to sleep."

He gave the child back to the beaming maidservant. "Is Agariste content?"

"She is tired but happy, master. The midwife says Agariste is very strong."

"She has borne me a fine son," Xanthippos said, "and well performed her duty." He would not see Agariste until she was purified, which could not be for some days; but his heart and hers would beat with the same elation. He felt closer to her in her absence now than he often did when she sat with her spinning in the open room off the court. He let the maidservant go back upstairs with her precious burden while he took the garland of olive which had been laid ready and went out to fasten it above the door himself. Had it been a girl, he would have waked the porter and bade him hang the white woolen bands to tell the neighbors. But it was a son.

Xanthippos finished hanging the garland and walked away down the street. His nerves were on edge from strain and lack of sleep. In the bustle about the child he was not wanted, while for the jostling and shouting of public life he was not ready. He needed to be alone, to think of his triumph.

There was a faint light in the eastern sky; but no one was yet stirring, save the country folk trudging in with market produce or those farmers who lived inside the city setting out to till their lots. Pretty soon the fish market would open, and better people would be getting up early to buy before the sun and the dust got into the booths. Xanthippos, walking quite steadily as though he had long made up his mind where he was going, went up the Acropolis rock on the western side, where rough steps cut in the stone marked the ascent.

There was nothing magnificent about the Acropolis yet, save its position in the heart of the city. Even the new stone temple, these twenty years abuilding, was not finished. Scattered around this were a number of mud-brick shrines, washed dingy white within and housing peculiar statues of great age and smoke-blackened altars. Out in the open stood a more recent image or two, a stone Athena standing straight with robe drawn sideways in one stiff hand and a set smile on her face. Similar objects were dotted about here and there as fancy had taken the Athenians from time to time, by no means all of them in very good repair and none particularly improved by the droppings of birds or the bits of thigh bones burned on the altars until they were more or less charred, and then thrown anywhere. Yet such as it was, the Acropolis was very holy and at this hour deserted. The time for sacrifice was not so pressing as the time for business.

Xanthippos halted near the base of a naked Apollo who stood planted on both feet with one set slightly forward, the conventional smile on his lean, taut features. There was something akin to Xanthippos's own mood in this male deity with the painted eyes and lips and the dark-blue hair. He looked up at Apollo, and the god looked straight over his head, while the sun peeped over the mountains and shone on the sea.

Xanthippos turned. He had been waiting for this moment. Spread out behind him lay the mountains with Pentelicon, a sharp and graceful triangle, in the midst, framed by Hymettus and the great mass of Mount Parnes, scored by ravines. Before him, four miles off, lay the narrow sea, all ripples, with the island of Aegina full in the center, as sharply peaked as was Pentelicon. Below lay Athens, a brown, irregular huddle of mud brick and tile, Athens the greatly loved. Xanthippos thought of his city less with conscious love than with real exasperation, yet it calmed him to see how still she lay in the center of that setting of mountain, island, and sea, as though her existence were as simple and eternal a fact as their own.

"The eyesore of Athens, eh?" said a voice in his ear. "Those pirates in Aegina!"

Xanthippos jumped. He did not like to be surprised

in this thoughtful mood, and most especially by that sharp upstart fellow Themistocles, whom he did not care for. "What brings *you* here?" he asked with an emphasis far from polite.

The fellow smiled. "I followed you, hoping for a private talk. For I think we two agree that if the conduct of public affairs is left to your noble kinsmen, we shall shortly find ourselves slaves of the king of Persia. There will be an end to our democracy then."

This was of all subjects the one Xanthippos least desired to discuss. For he did in fact agree with Themistocles, but to ally himself with that ambitious nobody was not to be thought of. As for democracy, if it brought to prominence adventurers like these with no real stake in the country, he was by no means sure it was worth having. He stared moodily across the sea at Aegina and said nothing.

"The Persian will not be content with less than burning the city and making slaves of us all," Themistocles insisted. "They say his servants remind him daily of Sardis."

"All Asia is in a turmoil with his preparations."

"Men say I am ambitious," Themistocles remarked. "But I have told nobody the extent of my ambition. I desire to become the greatest man in the first city of all Greece."

Xanthippos shrugged his shoulders. Athens was not the first city in Greece, nor had Themistocles in his eyes any claim to greatness. Such vast conceit he merely found annoying. To be sure, the fellow was clever . . .

"But I would die, if I must, to defend our city from the Persian king and would leave my ambitions to my children. So, I think, would you, Xanthippos."

In spite of himself, Xanthippos was impressed. The very selfishness with which he credited Themistocles increased this feeling. And he had been reminded once more of his newborn son. "Themistocles," he asked on an impulse, "do you believe that dreams foretell the future?"

"Who does not?" He spread his hands with a smile. "But to interpret dreams is seldom easy."

"That is so," Xanthippos agreed. "But I in my turn will tell you something. My wife Agariste dreamed she was brought to bed and bore a lion. And on the next night she was brought to bed indeed and bore me a son. I have been wondering what such a dream might mean."

"I wish it had been my wife," Themistocles exclaimed, "who dreamed that dream! What will you call such a son?"

"She is of better blood than I," Xanthippos said, "of the house of Alcmaeon. Her brother is Megacles, which means 'Great Glory.' I think to call this child Pericles, 'Exceeding Glory.'"

"Pericles . . . a good name for a lion." Themistocles smiled. "When I have made Athens the foremost city in Greece and have been rewarded by exile and disgrace after the manner of this people — well, then let your Peri-

cles prove himself a lion. I shall not grudge him glory if
he earns it."

"There is the Persian to be dealt with first," Xanthippos
answered.

# At the Gates of Sardis

## Asia Minor 480 B.C.

THE GREAT KING XERXES feasted in Sardis. The hall of
the governor's palace had been hung with tapestries
for the occasion and covered with carpets. The princes of
the Persians were drinking from beakers of gold, while
the very vessels for mixing wine and the flickering lamps
on stands down the long room were of hammered silver.
Nor was this fabulous treasure merely imported in the
train of Xerxes himself or borrowed for the occasion from
the governor's private store. All had been presented to
the king as a gift from his subjects. Indeed, should
Xerxes decide to feast again, a similar quantity of gold-
embroidered cloth and pearls and precious metals, not to
mention wine and perfumes, must be collected to present
to him once more. Small wonder that the Sardians, who
were present at the feast in inconspicuous numbers,

laughed loudly, but without mirth, and joined in the shouting with an anxiousness to please which could be detected. In all that splendid array nothing whatever had belonged to Xerxes before that night, save his gold and purple garments, the ivory throne on which he sat, and the special vessels in which his own water was mixed with the wine. For the king of Persia drank no water save from his native stream. This was carried with him wherever he went in his baggage train with its own bowls and beakers. All the rich carpets on the floor were a present from Sardis — and not only these carpets, but others on which the king had entered the hall. The king of Persia never set foot upon ground except in his native land. He traveled by chariot or litter, and the earth must be covered for him when he descended.

In appearance, the Great King Xerxes was a smaller man than his father had been. He was built more slenderly and looked less impressive. It was perhaps for this reason that his state was so much greater. The seal ring on his finger tonight was a huge emerald carved by a Greek artist whom the king thereafter had killed, lest he ever make a better. Jewels were sewed into his embroidered garments. Priceless perfumes scented his beard. King Xerxes did less hunting and more parading. When he traveled about his vast dominions, he never rode horseback. All this was not to say that Xerxes was not ambitious. Indeed, when he saw cause, he acted with vigor. The aging Darius had thought it good enough to send two of his generals to punish the Athenians. These, however, after landing on the coast had fought a battle with the Athenians and had been driven off. In fact, they had fled to their ships after losing many men. King Darius perceived that he had underestimated these Athenians. He had been ill, however; and in a year or two he had died, leaving his revenge to his son Xerxes.

It had not been easy for Xerxes to consolidate his power over the vastness of the Persian empire. Yet for all his love of display, he had shown qualities worthy of the son of a great ruler. New people had been raised to high positions, but older men had been handled with care. New family alliances had filled the king's harem. In a few years Xerxes sat firmly on his throne and could turn his attention to the one thing which still was lacking. All the princes of his house had been great warriors, and Xerxes thirsted as much as the rest for military glory. If he thought less of wielding a spear in the front rank of the horsemen and more of giving directions in the background, this was partly because the Persian operations had become too vast to be handled in the manner of his grandfather or his uncle, the conqueror of Egypt.

Since therefore Xerxes had an appetite for war, it was both his pleasure and his duty to avenge the defeats of his father by the Athenians. But a victory over so little a people could bring him scant credit. Darius had already paved the way. It would be for Xerxes to achieve the conquest of the whole of Greece.

He had undertaken his task with the thoroughness characteristic of his great father, and with an extravagance and sense of display all his own. Every part of his empire must contribute warriors. There were Ethiopians in leopard skins carrying Stone Age weapons. There were Indians in cotton clothes with bows and arrows of cane. There were nomad Scythians, Caspians, long-robed Arabians. There were men in wooden helmets, in leather skullcaps, plaited headdresses, foxskin hats, in the scalps of horses with mane and ears left on them. There were men in chain mail, leather, padded linen, bronze, men painted with chalk and vermilion. There were hook-nosed Easterners with olive complexions, brown men, black men, red-haired, blue-eyed men. They carried bows, spears, clubs, swords, scimitars, slings, and even lassos. There were men on horseback, men in chariots drawn by asses, men on camels. Every nation, be it useful or useless in war, had sent its contingent. The camp around Sardis was a hundred and eighty thousand strong, not counting the baggage with its trains of attendants, or the concubines of the great men in their litters, or the personal servants which every wealthy warrior took with him.

The heart of King Xerxes rejoiced in his splendor, yet his practical good sense laid no great value on the primitive peoples who made up much of his army. The backbone of his host were the Medes and the Persians, and in particular that picked band of ten thousand who were known as the Immortals. The instant that any Immortal died, the next man on the list filled up the ranks, so that they were always ten thousand. With the Immortals and his other disciplined troops, Xerxes would conquer. He would use the rest for forays, for garrison troops, or for overrunning and burning where he would not scatter his trained army. Xerxes had set Persian captains over the host and bade them mark out camp sites and muster their men for the march in some sort of order. With this he rested content and spent his last evening in Sardis feasting with his friends, not only Persians, for he was in little ways a more liberal man than Darius.

There was a man called Pythios who was wealthiest of all the Lydians. Indeed, except for the Persian, it would have been hard to discover a richer man throughout the world. This Pythios had already feasted the king and his whole army and also had offered his entire treasure in silver and gold for the king's war chest. Xerxes had been delighted, though even his magnificent ways could not spend the money that King Darius had laid up in gold and silver ingots. So fast did the tribute flow in from all over the world that even the mighty army which Xerxes had brought together could not exhaust it.

Not needing money, therefore, Xerxes was pleased to be magnificent. Instead of accepting the gift of Pythios, he further enriched him and swore friendship. Indeed he persuaded him to come with the army as far as Sardis, for Pythios was elderly and could hardly endure the strain of traveling farther.

To Sardis, therefore, Pythios came; and he now sat at meat with the king and his Persians. Xerxes was jovial and his kinsmen triumphant. The very vastness of the

army they commanded had overwhelmed their judgment. Moreover, like King Xerxes, they thought the Persians invincible. There were many toasts, therefore, and
much boasting and laughter. Only Pythios, who was an
older man and who knew Greeks, said nothing. The
king glanced at him once or twice; and had Pythios
really known Xerxes as the slaves and attendants did, he
might have felt alarmed. But after all, he was a gray-
beard, too old for fighting; and he was the king's sworn
friend. Even if it pleased him to be grave when the king
was merry, this might be passed over.

It nearly was passed over; but as Xerxes retired to his
apartments, he summoned Pythios with one of those curt
little nods he used for his slaves. "My friend," remarked the king in a displeased tone, "you do not re-
joice. Can it be you do not wish me well? I am loath to
believe it."

"Great King," old Pythios replied, "how should I lessen
your glory by any wish of mine? You know my devotion. I was silent because I had a parting request which
I desired but feared to make to the king."

"Make it," King Xerxes ordered. "It is granted already."

"I am an old man, O King," Pythios said, "and my
trading interests stretch far and wide, so that my business
is a burden to me. I have five sons to assist me, O King;
but all of them march in your army. Grant me therefore
just one, the eldest one. Let him remain to help me while
the others go with you to win you glory."

Then the king looked at him stony-faced. "So it was of your own affairs you thought and not of mine! You insolent slave! Is it not of my mercy that you yourself do not hobble to Greece with your wife in attendance? How dare you ask to keep back your son when none of my kinsmen are exempted from this war? Is this your devotion?"

Even the old man saw his danger now, and he flung himself at the feet of the king. "Grant me your pardon, King of Kings, because I am old and my tongue babbles foolishly. All that I have is the king's, both what he has given, and what I have offered him, and all beside."

The king looked coldly down on him. "I swore you friendship, and even now my oath shall protect you. Go free. But the eldest son whom you cherish — one half of his body shall be fixed on either side of the gate through which my troops march out from Sardis. Let the criers go through the host and tell them why this thing is done."

There was a silent bustle as some of the attendants went out without being named to do his bidding. And at the king's feet old Pythios, thinking of the four sons who were left, murmured, "The king's will is law."

# A Legend of Salamis

## Salamis 480 B.C.

*(As Recalled in Athens—462 B.C.)*

I WAS brought up on stories of Salamis. All our fathers and even a few older brothers had fought in that battle. By the time I was eight years old I could have recited the names of the Athenian ships and all of their captains, besides the size of the contingents of the various other Greeks and their battle stations. But about Themistocles himself I had heard little. There was a scandal connected with his name, some plot discovered of all places in Sparta. To be sure, the Spartans had hated Themistocles for reasons of their own; but then the Athenians in spite of what they owed him had not completely trusted him. Themistocles had fled, and being pursued with deadly rancor by many enemies, he had taken refuge in

Persia. Adding insult to injury, he had actually found
favor with the Great King by boldly claiming he had
tried to betray the Greeks in the Salamis battle. The
Athenians, though they themselves had forced him into
exile, never forgave this. Actually, they could hardly
deny him the glory of his victory; but they spoke of it
seldom, always adding that he was a traitor to Greece.
Thus it happened that until I was nearly twelve I never
discovered exactly what he had done and what we owed
him. Nor am I certain that I should ever have known,
had not our schoolmaster interrupted our studies that day
to tell us his story.

We had gone to school as usual, our slaves following
with our tablets and making sure we neither strayed nor
stopped to indulge in any childish game. We went
unwillingly, of course. We disliked not the poets, but
the long hours sitting on benches and learning by heart.
Our master Sicinnos was a good old man and by no
means as free with the rod as might have been proper.
We fidgeted under his eye, and we used to make idle
drawings on the wax of our writing tablets which we
hastily had to smooth out if he were coming. We were
always counting the hours till afternoon when we could
run and wrestle naked and talk like men to our trainers
while we scraped off dust and oil. Those who were older
among us counted even the days that they still had left
to go to school. As for Sicinnos, we never thought of him
as a person. He was a foreigner, a Thespian; and he had
at one time been rich. Now in his old age he had sunk to

the level of keeping school, we did not trouble ourselves why. He was our natural enemy and we his. But he might have been worse.

He was sitting in the schoolroom that day in the black garments of mourning and with his hair cut close. This was indecent, we thought. Surely a mourner need not inflict his sorrow on others. We ought to have had a holiday if the stingy old man could have spared the money. My neighbor on the bench whispered as much to me while we sat down. I pinched him, and he jumped. Our slaves settled themselves against the wall where they usually dozed through the lessons. Today they were muttering in their beards, while old Sicinnos looked at us without moving. Usually he would bustle about to set each one a task. The babble of the schoolroom with everybody learning his lines out loud would have arisen. Then he would have walked about for a while, keeping ears open for anyone who faltered in his learning.

Such was the first hour in school, but on this occasion Sicinnos merely watched us take our places, after which he said to us, "I wear this mourning for a great man who is dead."

He clasped his hands on his lap and looked at us in silence. We were awestricken and yet curious. Old Sicinnos had no patron that we knew, and there were not many for whom a stranger would mourn in black. Polemon, the eldest of us, put himself forward.

"Is it Cimon, master?"

"Is it Pericles?" asked Nicias, for the son of Xanthippos

was beginning to be talked about at that time.

He shook his head. "An even greater man has died in exile a very long way off. It is Themistocles. I once was his servant."

We had not known that Sicinnos had been a slave. It did not matter to us particularly, for slavery is a misfortune, not a disgrace. But the scandal which lingered about the name of Themistocles was still alive. I think all of us stared at our master with round eyes, beholding him for the first time as a man with a history. It was Ariston, the leather merchant's son and even then a loud-mouthed fellow, who came out flatly with what the rest of us thought. "Themistocles was a black traitor to Greece. I am glad he is dead."

Sicinnos shifted his eyes to where the slaves sat watching. I have since realized that these old men were spies on him as much as on us. It was his duty to teach us to read and write and learn the poets. It was theirs to see that he did so and to report if he did not. Therefore Sicinnos spoke rather to them than to us, realizing that by wasting any of our time he was at their mercy.

"Great men are always slandered, and Themistocles had the gift of arousing envy by sheer brilliance. Besides, he made an enemy of the Spartans, who never rested until they had hunted him down. Yet I was at Salamis with him, and I know what he did there for Greece. That battle was eighteen years ago when none of you were born. Shall I tell you about it?"

We chorused yes as a matter of course, only delighted

to waste a little school time in hearing a story.

"You all know the bay of Salamis, shut in by the island with a narrow strait at either end. And you know
how the sun goes down behind the hills of the Megarid.
Our ships lay at that western end of the bay, their sterns
in the sun. Since morning we had been ready, so that the
men had munched dry bread on the rowers' benches and
passed their skins of water and wine from hand to hand.
Now they leaned against their oars and dozed, hunched
forward, awaiting the signal to beach their ships and go
ashore to spend the night.

"While the men drowsed at their oars, the captains and
the watchmen stood on their poops to gaze at the Persian
muster, four miles away and gleaming black or red in the
declining sun. They were twice our numbers and had
also transports with them and merchant vessels of every
size, so that the whole afternoon had been needed for
their coming into their stations in the bay. Seeing us lie
ready, they did not back water into the shallows and go
ashore.

"The two fleets, then, lay looking at each other, while
the Athenian captains, who made up half our force, were
laying wagers about what they would do when it came
to the battle. They had watched the armies of the Persians cut down their olive trees to feed their campfires.
They had seen the pall of smoke which hung over Athens.
Such fugitives as made their way to us spoke of a destruction so complete that scarcely a stone lay piled on stone.

The Athenians had much to avenge and very little to lose.

"Not so the captains of the Southerners. All day long the Persian army had been moving south across the plain of Eleusis and into the Megarid like a column of ants. All the captains of the Peloponnesian states were looking over their shoulders at the army as often as they looked at the fleet ahead. Little was said between ship and ship, but boats were plying and meetings were being held of this group or that. Meanwhile, Themistocles paced uneasily up and down, watching who came or went, and guessing what was said. He could bear no more at last and left us himself. He was a wonderful talker; but no matter how brilliantly he spoke, he could not be as persuasive as the sight of that dark column moving south.

"When the sun was very low, we went ashore, and the captains called a meeting. The rowers clustered about their campfires in two groups with the Athenians and their friends all together, the Southerners apart. Our men were despondent, for the rumor was that we should move off south without giving battle.

" 'There is nowhere else so convenient for a fight as this,' I heard one argue. 'Here they cannot deploy their superior numbers.'

" 'Themistocles already told them that.'

"Another man spat in disgust. 'What can those Spartans know about ships with their miserable sixteen and their lubberly oarsmen? If our Themistocles were in the chief command . . .'

" 'If the Great King's fleet were dispersed, he would never adventure into the south of Greece with his army alone.'

" 'If we once refuse a fight, our fleet will break up. Those Southerners will never stick together.'

" 'Themistocles already told them that.'

"I could bear to hear no more. The fate of all of us hung on the meeting of captains, which must have been going on for an hour or more, since it was nearly dark. The longer it lasted, the stronger must be the vote for changing our plan. I left the campfire, round which I had no business lingering, and made my way to Themistocles's tent. I was his secretary and to some extent his body servant, so that after the meeting I must present myself in case I were needed.

"He was already there, or rather I ran into him at the entrance to his tent. He put his hand on my arm and said very quietly, his lips almost at my ear. 'Sicinnos? Good. Come outside, man. Quick! No noise!' He led me down towards the shore, avoiding the lights.

" 'They'll vote for moving south,' he said in the same low mutter. 'We are delaying it, but that's how they'll vote.'

" 'So we are lost, master,' I said in blank despair. You might imagine that being a Persian slave was not far different from being a slave here in Athens, but I knew better.

"He tightened his hand on my arm. 'I'm not defeated,' he told me. 'Why do you think I left the ship early? I've made preparations. Now, Sicinnos, I am turning to you.'

" 'I am your slave, master,' I told him. In truth I admired Themistocles and served him as well as I could. He shook me a little.

" 'Not my slave,' he muttered, unseen in the dark. 'I'll make you a free man, and make you a rich one, too, if you will save Greece.'

"I was sure he was not mad, yet I could not imagine what he desired. 'I'll do it,' I said. I would have done anything to gain my freedom.

" 'There's a boat beached round the point,' he whispered. 'A little coaster, one of my own. They're waiting for you. Take it straight across the bay and ask for the admiral of the Persians. Don't give your message to anyone less, or they'll not believe you. They'll have captives who'll recognize you as my attendant. See the admiral. Tell him Themistocles, the Athenian commander, seeks the favor of the Great King, to whose side he inclines. Tell him that therefore he sends word the Greeks will retreat south before dawn. But if the admiral will send a force round the island of Salamis to block the strait behind us, he will have us in a trap and may destroy us all. Tell him that.'

"I looked on him with awe, wishing I could see in the darkness whether his mischievous smile was on his face. 'You gamble for great stakes, my master. If we are beaten enclosed within the bay, not one will escape.'

" 'We should be no less ruined,' Themistocles said, 'if we were to retreat south. But here we shall win. We shall free Athens and in the end free Greece. I must be gone before I am missed at the meeting of captains. Did I say we are delaying the taking of votes?'

". . . So that's what Themistocles did." Sicinnos broke off. "That's how he saved Greece. Not many people would have thought of such a trick or had the nerve to risk it. But Themistocles, my children, was a man of boundless daring."

There was a silence which seemed very blank. Suddenly the story was over before we thought it had well begun. We were not ready to go back to our lessons.

"But didn't you get to see the Persian king?" Ariston asked. "My father saw him in the distance on his throne overlooking the bay where he sat next day to look at the sea battle."

Sicinnos smiled. "No, I never saw the king, except in the distance just as your father did. I saw his brother, who was the admiral of the fleet, a very tall man with a square beard in a tunic of purple and glittering all over with gold; but I dared not look at him, save out of the corner of my eye, since it is not the custom for humble folk to stare at Persian princes."

"But didn't you watch the battle next day?" I asked, disappointed. "My father was master of the *Thetis*. He said that when they knew they were surrounded, all the Athenians set up a great cheering."

"My father was in the *Calypso*," Nicias said. "My uncle told me that when our battle line started over the bay, our men were all singing that old song, 'Row, Odysseus.' "

"*Thetis* rammed three ships," I said. "She took the first one amidships and cut her almost in half. She beached the second. Then, though her own ram was broken and half her oars besides, she tackled a third one head on. My father led the boarding party while the ships were locked together. He said if the Persians had had more room to maneuver, nothing could have saved us. But our men fought like demons, he said. We had more to fight for than those Egyptians or the Asian Greeks who were slaves of the Persian. My father told me . . ."

Sicinnos shook his head at me gently. "It would hardly be fitting that I should waste your time in telling you stories of what I did myself or of what your fathers have described to you better than I. Our little coaster was at the back of the fight with all the merchantmen and transports of the Persians. Besides, as soon as we dared, we put off to sea." He shrugged. "We were thinking entirely of saving ourselves, since we were not armed. We had done our part."

I still felt very blank. "So that trick was all Themistocles did. It was clever of him, but I would rather have been in the *Thetis* with my father and boarded the enemy."

Sicinnos smiled. "You mean that it is better to fight

than to deceive. Perhaps it is, but Themistocles fought as well. I can tell you who saw him . . . your own attendant, Sosias. He was with the Persians."

I twisted around on the bench to stare at Sosias. Of course I had known he was a captive taken on that glorious day; but somehow or other it had never occurred to me that the view from his side might be of interest, too. Now to my amazement I saw that Sosias was setting down his staff in his deliberate way and preparing to speak. I could only remember what a beating I would get him at home if I revealed that he had been wasting the precious school hours telling stories. Sosias must have known that as well because his voice trembled a little and he spoke staring at me hard.

"Our ship was in the third rank," old Sosias said. "We were still maneuvering to get sufficient space, yelling at the Egyptian who was creeping up on our right hand and crowding our oarsmen. Over the shouting and the creaking of the leather in the oarlocks, the bumping of the waves, the clanking of armor, and all the other sounds of a ship at sea, we could hear the singing, or rather the yelling of the Greeks as they came closer. They charged across the bay in two irregular lines, evidently racing to see who could close with us first. Perhaps half a dozen of the swiftest drew out ahead, while the rest straggled after. Our front rank was in motion, too; but we behind them had hardly time to get under way before they were on us. There was a series of thunderous crashes as ships met, some brazen beak-to-beak, some sheering through the oars all down one side and tumbling the rowers from the benches into heaps, some crashing through the timbers. Our front rank, which had been moving more slowly than the Greeks, now came drifting back upon us, locked in combat. The Egyptian in a flurry ran into our oars. For many minutes we actually fought with our own side, cursing and shoving madly to get into the battle. The Greeks, meanwhile, came up as each one could and charged us headlong, disregarding the danger of ramming one another as they attempted to penetrate to the second rank or the third, which still lay motionless and would be easy prey. The roar of the battle rose all around us, deafening our rowers until they could scarcely hear the commands which were frantically given. More ships drifted against us, some half crippled; and soon the press around us was greater than ever.

"We won free at last, hoarse with yelling, running with sweat, with some oars broken and some rowers injured, although as yet we had not fought. A gap had opened; and by a frantic, well-timed effort we had got our men under way. In a few minutes we had actually room to maneuver and could choose whether to attack a crippled Athenian which was circling the huddle or to plunge once more into the hurly-burly, hoping to rescue some hard-pressed friend without being rendered helpless again. It goes without saying that we dug hard with our oars and rushed across the water to ram the Athenian head on.

"She had not been badly damaged. Her ram was still intact, and there was a cluster of armed men on her poop. But quite a number of her rear oars were dangling useless in the water. Thus slowed, she should be easy prey; but she showed no disposition to avoid our charge for all of that. Instead of dodging behind a pair of fighting ships, she steered right at us in lumbering defiance. Mad for the battle now, we disdained maneuver and trusted to our superior speed to break her up.

"We should have destroyed her, but before we came together, a trumpet signal rang out from her poop. With that, the trailing oars which had deceived us rose smartly with the rest. Before we could take in what had happened, the Athenian veered far more swiftly than we had given her credit for. She took us a little to one side, her great ram crashing through our timbers below the waterline, while ours cut useless sea."

"It was Themistocles," Sicinnos said, "who taught his men that trick."

Old Sosias nodded. "It was Themistocles who led the boarders across to cut us down, though the ship was sinking beneath him. He was a yelling devil in war, a terrible fighter. I threw away my weapon and jumped into the sea. No prisoners were taken in the heat of that battle, but I clung to a piece of wreckage and drifted onto the island. There I was taken and enslaved."

Sicinnos smiled at us. "You see, Themistocles was a warrior at need. Let me tell you one last little tale of what happened after the battle. When the victory had been won and King Xerxes had fled homewards, spoils were divided. At this time the chieftains held a meeting to decide which one among them had shown the most merit in the war. Then every ship's captain voted for himself, since every man's honor demanded that he say he had done best. But for the second prize, they named Themistocles."

# Themistocles in Sparta

## Sparta 478 B.C.

IN THE season following the last great battle which had expelled the Persians from Greece, the Ephors of the Spartans were sitting in their council house in conference. It was a dingy building, dark and wooden, with a floor of trodden earth and sparsely furnished with backless seats on which the old men sat. Nothing in their appearance denoted their position as chief magistrates of the most powerful people in Greece. Their cloaks were plain, shabby, and not too clean. Their hair and beards were shaggy, their horny feet dirty and bare. But they held their heads high and spoke, if not always with wisdom, at least with an air of quiet arrogance.

"This plan of the Corinthians is ingenious, I think," the oldest remarked. His tone suggested that ingenuity was a quality he despised, even while he found it useful.

The second Ephor nodded grave approval. "Considering the destruction which the Persian wrought in Athens," he pointed out, "one might have imagined that the Athenians would have been kept busy for years. Why, the temple of Athene, which they have been so long in building, was thrown down in heaps of rubble. The city walls were destroyed. Tombstones and shrines were uprooted. Only such houses as had been the headquarters of Persian generals were left standing. Olive trees and vines were cut for fuel and the land turned into a desert."

"New vineyards," the third reminded him, "will not bear for four years, new olives not for twenty. In the meanwhile, the Athenians have their ships and many ruined men, who are greedy for plunder."

"It would never have been fitting," objected the fourth, "to send our own army north. Even as it is, our Spartan youth is infected with foreign customs. And what does it matter if the Persian rules in the North. We do not trade."

"Neither was it fitting," the youngest leaned forward urgently, "for the Athenians to go and make these conquests without us. Have we not always been the leaders of Greece?"

The oldest nodded. "Even the Corinthians are jealous of Athens now," he said. "They fear her trade.".

"Then let the Corinthians themselves send envoys to Athens and forbid them to fortify their city again. Why should we fear what the Athenians do? We are the Spartans."

"We fear nobody," said the oldest solemnly. "But we take the lead. It is for us to propose to the Athenians that instead of rebuilding their wall they should join in forcing all cities north of the Peloponnese to tear down their own. How can the Corinthians put forward such a plan, seeing that they themselves have fortifications? But we Spartans who, as all the world knows, protect ourselves only by the stout shields of our men . . . we can make the suggestion."

"Give the order," corrected the second Ephor flatly.

The oldest smiled and stroked his beard. "To be sure, if they refuse us we will send an army. But open and defenseless as they are, they will not dare refuse. Why therefore order? The Corinthians suggest we give our demand a decent appearance. We may say that if the Persian returns, he must not be able to use the northern towns as strongholds. And when he does come, they may all of them migrate to the Peloponnese."

"Unwalled, the Athenians will lie at our mercy forever," the third Ephor said with relish. "For all their boasting about the sea battle at Salamis, they never could meet us in war."

"Very clever!" The tone of the youngest Ephor certainly suggested that cleverness was not much admired.

"These Corinthians pride themselves on being clever," sneered the third.

"The Corinthians grow rich and corrupt through

trade," the eldest agreed. "But they look to us. The Athenians ought to do so, too. We will send envoys to make this proposition."

The second laughed. "There'll be long faces in Athens."

All five nodded, and looking upon one another, they smiled.

The Spartan message was indeed received at Athens with consternation. Many were the secret discussions between the leaders of state. Unfortified as they at present were, they dared not defy the Spartans. Yet never to build a wall meant never to be independent. The Athenians temporized. They sent the Spartan envoys home with compliments and proposed to dispatch an embassy of their own to discuss the matter and arrive at some agreement.

The Spartan envoys soon returned home and reported to the Ephors. Spartan training in simplicity did not ever tend to make them particularly trustful of other people. However, all seemed satisfactory, since hardly had the Spartan envoys had time to reach their homes before Themistocles set out in person to discuss the problem with Sparta.

He traveled in state, and he took his time. Even the Corinthians, through whose territory he passed, were aware that Themistocles was the real savior of Greece. They could not but honor him when he traveled as an envoy with his slaves, his tents, his baggage wagons, and all his splendor and parade. They did not like him; and

yet he was so smooth, so deaf to snubs, so determinedly
pleasant that they were put on their mettle and forced
to be gracious. They entertained him, and Themistocles enjoyed himself so well that he lingered. He was
in no hurry; for his fellow ambassadors were detained in
Athens, as he said, on urgent business. In this fashion
Themistocles passed slowly through the Peloponnese and
came to Sparta.

He pitched his tents on the Spartan plain and went to
see the Ephors unattended and dressed in the Dorian
fashion like the Spartans, though if the truth be told
somewhat fresher and cleaner.

"Do the Athenians agree or don't they agree to leave
their city unwalled?" the Ephors demanded. Spartan
manners were purposely abrupt, and a certain rudeness
was called simplicity there. Themistocles smiled.

"You make the whole matter too easy. There is the
question of Thebes and other cities which at present are
fortified. The Athenians have much to propose and
much to discuss, but until my two colleagues have finished their business at home, I dare not treat with you.
The Athenian people have by no means granted me permission to settle their policies alone. Our democracy is
too jealous to endure that any one man should have such
power."

"If you can't discuss it, man, then why did you come?"

"To see Sparta!" He flung out a hand. "Here is the
celebrated unwalled town dedicated to the practice of
simple virtue! Here each lives like the rest! Here money

buys nothing! When I was appointed envoy to such a place, why should I delay to set out thither? Let my colleagues come on as soon as they can. I want to see Sparta."

The oldest of the Ephors looked at him with unfriendly suspicion. It stood to reason no doubt that a man like Themistocles must admire Sparta. Everybody envied the Spartan way of life, though strangely no one had imitated it so far. Still, this matter of the Athenian walls was supposed to get settled. Moreover, Themistocles had the name of being clever and not by any means straightforward in his methods. "How soon do you expect your colleagues?" the Ephor asked sourly.

"Seven days, ten days, who knows? To tell the truth, Aristides, whom the Athenians so greatly trust, is still abroad. Abronichos, the other ambassador, fell sick of a fever. If he does not recover before Aristides returns, they will send someone else."

The Ephor nodded. At least the Athenians would be forced to act in good faith as long as Themistocles himself was in Spartan hands. They would not sacrifice their greatest man to Spartan wrath. All the same, the delay was a nuisance.

It appeared Themistocles had a favor to ask. He wanted to eat with one of the communal messes like a real Spartan. He had come ready with his rations for the month — a bushel of barley, eight pitchers of wine, five pounds of cheese, two and a half pounds of figs, and a few relishes. He wanted to taste the Spartan black

broth, so widely famous for its revolting qualities that no
one was said to like it who had not bathed from youth in
the river Eurotas. But Themistocles managed to enjoy it,
or so he claimed. He praised abstemiousness, barked
his shins cheerfully as he walked home in the dark without a torch, as Spartans did to improve their night vision.
He picked up a bundle of Spartan money, which was
nothing more than iron rods, too heavy to carry about
and therefore of little use. He laughed gaily and promised to recommend this currency to the Athenians. In
the mess hall, he did not talk about himself, nor yet endure the foolish conversation that was usual. Instead, he
drew his fellows out, professing, for instance, a curiosity
to know what it felt like to be one of the picked youths
sent out by the Ephors to police the serfs and spread ter-
ror among them by sudden assassinations. What was it
like, he asked, to marry a woman one had never seen, to
visit her only by stealth and in the dark . . . in fact
never to see her until the first child was born? To every
such question he wanted answers; and no matter what
they were, he lifted hands in admiration. Even when a
dirty, barefoot, half-starved boy was caught stealing from
the mess and brutally flogged, Themistocles said nothing
as he watched the child take the blows without a cry.
When they let him go limping off, the men guffawed.

"Disgraceful!" one of them said. "He'll do better next
time."

"I thought he looked hungry," remarked Themistocles
mildly.

The Spartan messmates had lost their awe of Themistocles by now, and they treated him as a rather dull pupil in Spartan customs. They grinned.

"Hungry! Of course he's hungry. We keep our boys hungry. Teaches them to forage for themselves like real campaigners."

"Yet you beat him."

"He got caught, didn't he? That beating was nothing to what he'll get from his Youth Leader. Don't imagine he was stealing to fill his own belly. He was under orders. He'll be lucky if he eats today at all after such a performance."

There was a silence.

"I had heard a tale or two," Themistocles said. "But there is nothing like seeing with one's own eyes. You are an extraordinary people."

The Spartan swaggered. "We're brought up right."

"Indeed I see you are," Themistocles agreed.

The very next day the Ephors sent for him about a rumor the Corinthians had passed on that the Athenians were hard at work building a wall.

"Impossible!" Themistocles protested.

"If you play fast and loose with us," said the Ephor bluntly, "it'll cost you your life."

"But of course!" He shrugged his shoulders. "I too have had a message. Aristides is due in Athens in a day or two. Then nothing need prevent my colleagues from coming to settle this problem. In the meantime, I would like to see how you train your children. I have a son of my own who is, I fear, spoiled. I command the Athenians, my wife commands me, and the boy commands my wife. You may imagine the embarrassment this causes! Indeed I have much to learn from Spartan methods." He was laughing as he spoke, and none of the Ephors knew if he meant what he said. Yet as far as the matter of the Athenian walls was concerned, he would not dare deceive them. No one, least of all Themistocles, would sacrifice his life.

After this, Themistocles spent much of his time studying the education of the boys, who were taken from their parents at the age of seven years and put in barracks. He inspected these buildings, which were bare and bleak. He watched the boys drilling. They looked thin and wretched, he said, with their close-cropped hair, bare feet, and single garment. They were toughened by not being allowed baths, by sleeping on pallets of reeds which they pulled with their bare hands from the river Eurotas. Their Youth Leaders beat them savagely for the slightest offense, while the elders watched with approval. Themistocles quoted the Sybarite who had said, "I no longer wonder at the Spartan contempt for death. It would be far better to die a thousand times over than to live such a life." But though he laughed himself, neither the Youth Leaders nor the elders who were looking on thought this remark funny.

Themistocles left the boys alone after that and went to watch the girls, taking with him his guards. It had by now occurred to the Ephors that he might plan to slip away. Once more the Corinthians had sent a message to say that the Athenians, man, woman, and child, were toiling to build walls. Once more Themistocles had shrugged this assertion off. The Corinthians were jealous. If they could create bad blood between the Athenians and the Spartans, they would not scruple to do it. Aristides had been delayed by contrary winds, but soon the embassy of the Athenians would give satisfaction. The Ephors then compromised by setting guards, whom Themistocles treated as though they were guards of honor. As for escaping, nothing seemed further from his mind. He watched the girls drilling in their little short tunics, running, jumping, even wrestling. "Our daughters are too much shut up at home," he said. "We think it shocking that they should not be timid and shy, and yet sometimes we forget they ought to be healthy." Then he called over the girl who had won in the footrace and asked her name.

"Doris." The girl looked him full in the eye, by no means embarrassed by his curious gaze or her scanty dress, yet like all Spartans unwilling to waste a word in giving an answer.

"Tell me, Doris, then, what is the purpose of all these sports of girls? You do not go to war."

"They train us to bear healthy sons for the state."

"Oh, sons. Would you not rather bear a daughter, seeing that boys are taken from you so young, while girls stay with their mother?"

Doris frowned. "The state needs men."

"And mothers of men." But this was too difficult for Doris, especially with the Spartan guards looking on. She took refuge in rudeness.

"None of you foreigners understand us. You're too soft."

Themistocles smiled good-humoredly and told his guards that Spartan women made wonderful nurses and he wished he had one for his own children. Since, however, nursing was a slavish, low-class profession, the guards did not take this as a compliment. They roundly told him that he was sent for to the Ephors. There was a message once more about the walls of the Athenians.

"Impossible!" said Themistocles again, but he went. The Ephors were very angry.

"You dare deceive us!" they greeted him. "You will repent it."

"But I do not dare. How could I?" asked Themistocles mildly.

"The Corinthians . . ."

"Are accusing us out of mere malice, as I already told you."

"The Corinthians," the eldest Ephor pointed out, "may hate the Athenians, but they are allies of ours. What possible motive could they have for offending us by false information?"

Themistocles shrugged his shoulders. "If you don't believe me, at least you should see for yourselves. Choose Spartans whose word you may respect, and send them to look. I'll wait here gladly. I want to see the festival of

Artemis in which you whip boys in front of the wooden image to see how much pain they can take without crying out. My friends here tell me," he nodded at the guards, "that I'll never understand Sparta until I see that sight. It's magnificent, they say."

The Ephor nodded. Themistocles talked so much and was so plausible that he hardly knew what to say. "Our boys," he agreed, "are trained to endure. We are proud of them."

"Is not that wooden image," Themistocles asked, "reputed to be the one which Iphigenia, Agamemnon's daughter, brought from Tauris? Strangely, we have an image for which we make the same claim, but we do not whip boys in front of it. Our little girls between five and ten dance a bear dance, a sort of game, in honor of it."

The Ephor had not been listening to this. It was not the custom of the Spartans to show interest in other people's ways, most especially in the games of their little girls. He had taken advantage of Themistocles's garrulousness to make up his mind. "We'll send two envoys to see what the Athenians are doing. If they're building, it will be the worse for you, Themistocles."

He laughed without a care in the world. "I am in your hands."

The festival of Artemis came and went. By now the envoys which the Spartans had dispatched should have returned, but they lingered . . . doubtless, as Themistocles said, intending to hurry Aristides and Abronichos by waiting for them. When, however, these two ambassadors at last appeared, the Spartans were not with them. They pitched tents by Themistocles and very naturally came to consult with him before meeting the Ephors.

"It's done," Aristides told him. "Not finished, but defensible. We used the stones of the temple, tombs, inscriptions, all the rubble except the actual images of the gods. We worked day and night. It's not a handsome wall, made with such materials, but it's strong."

"Watch the Ephors when they hear," Themistocles said. "These horrible people! I do not call myself squeamish, Aristides. If a man must be tortured or executed for good reason, I'll look on. But they beat boys here, they actually beat them to death. I watched them kill two at the altar of Artemis, just trying to see if they could make them cry out. . . . Ah, well, you admire them."

"They're honest."

"And stupid. Give me a man who can think."

Aristides laughed. "It was lucky they did not."

"It was easy to make fools of them," Themistocles said, "and so I despise them."

He made no effort to disguise this feeling when the envoys were received, not merely by the Ephors but by the Council of Elders. Constituting himself spokesman for his fellows, he threw off all pretense and spoke with defiance.

"The Athenian people instruct us to inform you that their city is now fortified. Henceforward if the Spartans put forward proposals, they should do so well understanding that the Athenians are capable of making up their own minds without advice. It was not after consultation with the Spartans that we abandoned our homes to the Persian and betook ourselves to our ships. Yet by so doing we saved Greece. We Athenians are now your free and equal allies. In common fairness we claim the means of defense as well as you."

There was a great hubbub when he had finished speaking. All of the elders were in a rage at having been deceived by his barefaced lies. It was left, however, to the eldest of the Ephors to retort, "Themistocles, you think yourself very clever, but we Spartans have a short way to deal with people who deceive us."

Themistocles laughed outright at that, and he said, "Remember your envoys, those two noble Spartans whom you sent to see for themselves! Be sure the Athenians will keep them until I return, and anything you may do to us will be done to them."

Then the Spartans saw that they had been completely outwitted, and there was nothing left for them to do but to vent their anger in threats.

"You are too pleased with yourself, Themistocles," the Ephor told him. "Do not forget that we Spartans are the strongest state in Greece. We have also many allies. The time will come when we shall hunt you down and drive you out of Athens and all Greece."

Themistocles looked around on his enemies. He knew them to be hard, determined men who would never forgive him. He was used to making enemies, however, and to taking risks. The Spartans might destroy him in the end, or they might not do so. Meanwhile, he would not even attempt to win their forgiveness. He said, "You are warlike, O Spartans, and you think yourselves all-powerful. You have not begun to see what the Athenians can do. Now that the Persians have been defeated, you are the same as before — the same as you were, the same as you always will be. We Athenians, whom you despise as traders and amateurs, are a new people. We have beaten the greatest host that man ever saw. Now we know there is nothing we cannot achieve if we desire to. When we have made Athens the queen of the seas, the school of all Greece, the envy of nations, then, Spartans, pull us down if you still have the power."

"You boast, but deeds count more than talk," the Spartan answered.

"So they do, and so they will. Keep your eyes on the Athenians. Our victory against the Persians will yet look small beside the future. We Athenians will lead the world; and I, Themistocles, shall lead the Athenians."

"The man is a drunken fool and no more." The Ephor shrugged. "Let him go for the present, since no man's life is worth two Spartans. We will remember this day when the time comes to be avenged."

# Athenians of the Golden Age

## 480–431 B.C.

# The Athenian

## Athens 470–458 B.C.

IT WAS NOT until he won at the Thesea, which were the games for young men and boys, that Criton's ambition allowed him to dream of a silver cup at Marathon or a prize in the games of Eleusis. He dared not aspire to the black-figured jars of oil from the sacred olive trees which were given the victors at Athene's contests. Criton had won at the long jump and in the throwing of the javelin and discus. But he had not won at the wrestling, and in the footrace he had not placed at all. In fact, had not the rules of the youths' pentathlon been laxer than the men's, he would never have qualified to compete in the finals. He took his reward, therefore, with becoming modesty and blushed when spoken to by Pancleon himself, who had won the footrace at Olympia and was famous throughout Greece.

"You lost that race with your start," Pancleon told him severely. "You should swing your arms so!"

Criton shuffled with embarrassment as he promised that he would practice the swing. The start of the footrace with feet placed side by side was very awkward, and much depended on the leap with which the athlete fell into his stride. Yet Criton's trouble lay less in technique than in a simple lack of speed. In the actual presence of the great man, he dared not admit this.

"I'll come and put you right," Pancleon told him. "No hope of qualifying at Marathon with such a disgraceful performance."

He walked off, leaving Criton so much terrified at the thought of displaying his shortcomings that even the praise of his friends, the delight of his father, and the very compliment of being noticed by Pancleon at all did not elate him.

Only three days after the Thesea, Pancleon appeared at the gymnasium, tore Criton's whole performance to shreds, and made him practice his start for an hour on end. He shouted at him, borrowed the trainer's stick and poked, and finally lost patience and slashed at him when his timing still was awkward. All this was very unpleasant, and so was the running in armor which Pancleon then prescribed to strengthen his muscles. By the time he was dismissed, he could only stagger panting to the portico and flop down to get his breath, putting off the effort of scraping off sweat and oil and dust, of bathing and massage.

All of the young men had gone but three. In the course of their military training, which had taken up the last two years, this group had formed of hard-and-fast friends who had kept together on the march, shared their fatigues, or sat around campfires and talked until the stars grew pale in the sky. They had waited for Criton and began to revive him with sips of wine and water. Presently Alcias took the scraper and began to work on his back, whereat they started to press him about what the great man had said.

"Did Pancleon tell you to enter for Marathon next spring?" Theocritos asked him.

The flush which had just been dying in Criton's cheeks came up again. "Well, after a fashion . . ." He bent over, rubbing at his legs to hide his confusion.

"Exactly what did he say?" demanded Alcias laughing. "It hardly sounded at this distance like a compliment, I can assure you."

"Oh, it wasn't," agreed Criton in haste. "Excepting . . . but I don't suppose he meant that anyway. Indeed, he could not have."

"I am losing my patience," Hippias drawled, stretching himself. "Presently I shall throw you in the dust again and make you clean yourself over."

Criton, who was half a head taller than Hippias and broader as well, grinned at him. "Oh, have it your way.

I'll tell you exactly what Pancleon said if I can remember. He was swearing at me mostly . . . 'You blockhead, you clodhopper, you! Can't you pick your feet up?' Then he said, 'You think the discus and the javelin and the jump will give you a victory, don't you? Well, they're not good enough if you fail in the footrace.' Then he swore at me some more and said, 'If you can't win the footrace at Athenian games, you fool, how do you imagine you're going to place at all when you get to Olympia?' *Olympia!* Then he hit me a crack with that stick because my timing was wrong, and he swore at me some more. But that's what he said."

There was a silence.

"Olympia!" Hippias breathed. "I knew he would not take the trouble to come and look at you for nothing. Not Pancleon."

"There hasn't been an Athenian to win at Olympia since Pancleon's own time," said Theocritos quietly. "Don't misunderstand me if I say I envy you, Criton."

"And I," agreed Hippias, who was to give his life for Athens in the victory of the Eurymedon two years later. "To be an Athenian and then to win at the games! I do not grudge Criton the glory — why should I do that? But the achievement!"

"To show the world," Alcias said, "that we Athenians . . . oh, that we are what we are . . ." Alcias was later to produce the plays of Euripides three times and score one win.

"I don't believe Pancleon meant it," Criton protested,

alarmed by the responsibility laid on his shoulders of glorifying the fairest city on earth. "I'll never make a runner, and he as good as told me so. But if I fail in the footrace, I'll not win."

"You'll not fail," Hippias told him. "Pancleon will see to that. And don't you remember how we used to tell ourselves we were going to make Athens the envy of Greece?"

They had thought of themselves as caught up in a torrent of achievement, not as bestowing any glory by their singlehanded efforts. Criton felt the difference and was afraid, but all he said was, "Ah, we'll see what Pancleon does. I rather imagine he'll waste no effort on me. Mere words mean nothing."

Next day Pancleon was back, and the next day thereafter. Without precisely discussing the matter, he soon had it settled that Criton should be worked half to death, and woe betide him if he came a few minutes late or pleaded illness. Pancleon demanded his whole time and was soon interfering with how he dined and where he spent his evenings. That summer Alcias was sent to Sicily by his father, who had business interests there. Hippias and Theocritos spent more time in the porticoes discussing the new learning than in watching athletics or taking part therein. They were always glad to see Criton, and they cheered him at Marathon next year, where he did not win. Pancleon was angry and said that he would have to practice harder. He had not the leisure to sharpen his wits with his friends; and in the year following, Hippias went abroad with the fleet and died at Eurymedon.

Criton won at Marathon that year, and he won at Eleusis. In the year following, which was the year of the great games of Athene, he won the pentathlon, coming first in all five events. Next he went into training for the Pythian games at Delphi. He missed Delphi through an accident to his foot at the long jump, and had to mark time for two years while he was waiting for the sacred Olympian year. Meanwhile, however, the people of his district drafted him to serve against the island of Thasos, which was seeking to withdraw from the Athenian alliance.

Criton went on the campaign as though on holiday. The relief from the monotony of dust and sweat and sun and physical action was greater because of the sea voyage and because there was blockading rather than fighting. He sat around campfires, as he used to do in his younger days before the glory of Athens had descended like a weight on his broad shoulders. For a month or so he was deliriously happy, though the talk was different, and the people had changed. They were much wittier. They knew the choruses of that young poet, Sophocles. They talked about physical science and theories of matter, which they said were being discussed in Sicily. They did not ask Criton his opinion, but assumed he had none, which was in fact the case. When he put his word in on subjects which he knew, they sometimes looked bored. He soon found it better to sit quiet and drink things in.

He became fascinated, confused, excited, and very lonely. At the end of the summer, he was glad to get back to good old routine with Pancleon saying he must make up for lost time by practicing harder.

The sacred year was announced in July, and for ten months of it the candidates had to train under special rules. Even Pancleon conceded that Criton worked hard, for now that his supreme test was drawing near, he fell into panic. Who was he to challenge the greatest athletes of every state in Greece? Not even Pancleon could turn him into a runner of that class, and both of them knew it. Would it not be better for his city's fame that he should not go at all?

Of course he went. Indeed, when the eleventh month came round, he had no alternative. His father and brother had put all business aside to accompany him. His uncle and cousins would be following in the sacred month to see the games. Nor was he alone. In the Athenian party there was Callias, who had entered his horses for the chariot race; and there was his jockey; and Glaucon entered for the wrestling match alone; Diocles for the running in armor; and a surly, broken-nosed brute called Molon for the boxing, who was expected to win. There were two or three for the boys' sports besides, so that what with all of them and their attendants they were over fifty; and their setting out from Athens was very public. Almost as festive was their progress through the towns that lay in their way, the more particularly as Callias was a rich man and made great parade.

The arrival at Elis was grim reality again, as was the settling for a month of training routine. But now for the first time Criton really measured himself against the athletes of Greece. His heart sank like stone. In the javelin throwing, to be sure, and in the discus and jump he was one of three. But in the footrace there were eight or ten who were faster than he; and Pancleon had told him if he were not in the first six, he would not qualify to enter the other events at all. Peison of Corinth, who had won the pentathlon in the last Olympiad, was favored for the footrace and perhaps for the long jump as well, while in the wrestling he was agreed on all hands to stand an even chance.

This much Criton perceived in ten days; and for the month of his training at Elis, try everything that he would, he gained no ground. Rather he wondered if he were not slipping as Pancleon grew louder and more insistent with him day after day.

That month went by too fast. They formed the festal procession; and the judges of the games led them out from the township of Elis to the sacred precinct of Zeus, which was at Olympia. Two days they took to get thither, making sacrifices and singing, winding slowly up the bank of the Alpheus River, appearing finally in sight of the vast throng which had come from every city in the time of the sacred truce to watch the games.

Now the tension among the athletes rose to fever pitch, excited by the frenzied roar of the people and the yells of the hucksters from their booths. The plain was seething, overflowing from the colonnades to tents or huts and thence to the bare grass, where hordes of people spent the night on the ground and feasted frugally on bread they had brought with them, buying a handful of nuts, dried figs, or little wilted onions, and a measure of wine well diluted with Alpheus water. Men were massed all along the sacred way. The tents of the embassies which the states had sent to Olympian Zeus were almost thrown down as people surged around them, pushing to get a better view of the procession. This went into the precinct of Zeus, where the dazzling temple of the Olympian stood, so new that its sculpture — by an Athenian hand — was not yet finished. Dotted around stood statues preserving for all time the names of victors whose deeds had glorified their native city. Of many competing, how few in every year achieved such honor!

Criton looked pale, even green. The tedious walking at an almost dawdling pace was physical idleness and torture to his high-strung nerves. Tomorrow there would be the oath-taking and the long-drawn-out procedures of formal entry. Then in the afternoon, his father and kinsmen were offering sacrifice. There would be an endless wait for their turn at an altar.

There was. That first day of the feast appeared interminable. It was in fact the day of the market, not of the games. Jugglers and acrobats appeared, performing marvels. Peddlers cried new notions. Poets gave readings. Men of learning expounded new ideas in eloquent speeches. Sudden meetings with long-lost friends made

little swirls of excitement among the jam-packed crowds.
Everybody was noisy, hot, exultant. Even Pancleon lost
his head and boasted with the rest at the little banquet
which consumed the meat of Criton's sacrifice. It was
fortunate that the rules did not permit the competitors to
eat at this time of day, or else the morsels would surely
have stuck in Criton's throat. He was dizzy with head-
ache, sick with nerves. The very muscles of his face were
stiff with smiling. He would be beaten tomorrow in the
first heat of the footrace, and his friends would fall silent.

He got up to slip away. There were other little ban-
quets for other competitors dotted everywhere in tents
and booths, those of the Athenians being naturally nearest the embassy of Athens. He might just possibly
be thought to have gone somewhere else to offer good
wishes.

He bumped into someone as he went out and was
stopped with a hand on his arm. "Criton! Don't you
know me with this beard?"

He felt the sudden surprise of real pleasure. "Alcias!
I never thought you would come. We don't meet now."

"I broke my leg in Sicily," Alcias said, "and as you see,
I'm lame. As for you, you're bigger than ever. You've
changed besides."

Criton thought it was Alcias who had changed, but in
pity he did not say so. "It was good of you to take the
trouble."

"For myself, I'd not have done it," Alcias admitted. "You see, we've grown apart. But I promised Hippias."

"Hippias!" Criton had hardly thought of Hippias for two years, or perhaps more, though once he had cared for him more deeply than the others.

"Hippias was sorry when he saw you were dropping out," Alcias explained. "He thought that for the sake of our city you were missing something. So he made us promise that when your time came to win, we'd at least go and see. But then Theocritos — his father's captaining a warship this year, and Theocritos can't be spared. So I came alone."

"It was good of you, Alcias," Criton said again. He was really moved, but he had become unused to expressing finer shades of feeling among men like Pancleon. "It was good of Hippias, too. But you might have saved yourself the trouble of coming. I'm not going to win."

"Hippias dreamed you would win," said Alcias, "and he dreamed he could not get there, no matter how hard he tried. That's why he was anxious that we should promise to go. He knew you would win."

Criton felt a strange sensation. At the sacrifice this afternoon they had told him that the omens were very favorable. But then priests could be bribed; and if they were not, they would be anxious at a time like this to encourage everybody. A dream, and from Hippias, four years dead, meant something more. The color came flooding back into his cheeks, just in the same fashion that it used to do when he blushed; and he said, "To be an Athenian and then to win at the games! Remember, Alcias? And you said . . ."

"To show the world that we Athenians . . . Yes, I remember. It's not so long ago, and I'm glad to have come."

Criton knew he would win as soon as the lots were drawn next day for the footrace. Peison of Corinth and a half-dozen more of the best runners were all in the last heat, which meant not only that they would have to run twice in quick succession, but that no less than four of them would never qualify to run in the finals at all. As for himself, he drew the first heat, with no necessity for so much as running full out. When the time for the finals came up and he could measure the field, he thought there were seven or possibly eight of them who could still surpass him. Some, however, were winded and panting. Besides, it was his day.

One started too soon and was disqualified. One slipped at the turn. Criton for his part ran as never before and took third place. This was sufficient. It was easy to win at the javelin after that, and then at the discus. Peison beat him by a bare inch at the long jump, after having won the footrace. It was the wrestling, therefore, in which Criton did not excel, which must be decisive. It was not that either need win the wrestling bouts, but that in the course of them one must defeat the other. Luckily they were matched first, since Peison as the older and far more powerful man would surely out-

last him. Peison wrestled by the Argive school in which
Criton had also been trained, and which he had practiced
quite openly at Elis. In secret, however, Panclcon had
provided a Sicilian who had instructed him for the past
year in the new science of offering one's opponent holds
to his undoing. This was a risky way to treat an Argive
expert, who was fast and hard enough to take advantage
of any grip he was given. Criton's nerves, however,
were now ice-cool. He had the judgment to score one
fall and suffer two, letting Peison, who knew himself the
better man, see victory only one single fall away. Then
Criton offered a wrist, appeared to slip, turned, threw up
the other arm, and Peison went flying. So sudden was the
motion that it seemed mere accident, and the crowd
booed.

Peison was up in a moment, surprised, but warier, suspicious by training and conscious that another mistake would be his ruin. They came at each other, heads butting. Criton offered a chance for a body grip, but Peison refused it. This time he would choose his own method and would make certain.

Greatly daring, Criton slipped in the sand again and dropped his hands as if to regain balance. Like a striking snake, Peison lunged out for the grip on his neck. He missed because in the foolhardiest movement seen at Olympia in living memory, Criton had thrown himself right under Peison's guard to reach for his leg. He thereby exposed himself to such a variety of falls that wiser people would spend the next ten years reminding him of them. In fact, it was a boy's trick, carried out with hard precision and successful because it defied every regular rule. Peison staggered, caught vainly at Criton's hair, and went flat over. After that it did not matter who won the wrestling finals. They would crown Criton. They were going to bind a fillet around his hair and to crown him with olive cut from the sacred tree with a golden sickle. When the trumpets called for silence, they would announce him as winner of the pentathlon. Criton, the Athenian! The cheers of the vast concourse would make the horizon ring with "The Athenian!"

The last three days of the feast passed in delirium. Criton was feted and wondered at and extolled until his head reeled. After that he was cheered from Olympia to Elis and back through all the cities of Greece past which he had come. The very magistrates of Athens came out of the city to welcome him home. The people escorted him to the temples and gave thanks. They granted him a prize in money, a seat of honor at festivals, the right of joining in the banquet daily offered the leaders of state. Theodotus, the poet, wrote a hymn. Myron, the sculptor, made a statue entitled "Criton the son of Critias, who won the pentathlon in the games at Olympia." It did not add, "The Athenian," and Criton never missed it. So many praises had been showered on him saying simply, "Criton."

He thought that the flattery had not gone to his head; and he took credit to himself for going to Pancleon and saying, completely as man to man, "I've got some new notions that I want to try in training. You know I was favored by the gods in the footrace this year. That won't happen again."

So the old round started again, and some of his notions improved his technique. He won at Delphi; and when the sacred year came round once more, he won at Olympia. But whereas the first time the very skies had echoed "Athenian," what rang in his ears now was simply, "Criton." When he returned to Athens, he and Pancleon seemed to dwarf all other men by the greatness of their glory.

He started to train again, although the pentathlon with its five events was considered a young man's game. Few had ever won it three times. The effort to do so took up most of his waking hours, while time stood still.

Time had stood still many years for him, while
time in Athens rushed by on the wings of the wind. Already at Thasos the new young men had left Criton behind. Now these were planning, creating, fighting,
dying for Athens, as the imperial city climbed up to
dizzying greatness, undertaking so many tasks at once
that the whole world marveled. In recent years even
younger men had arisen, still more eager, while dazzling
opportunities dawned and limitless power to do the impossible in that glorious age seemed granted.

No one could have lived in such an era without feeling
its challenge after a fashion. Even Criton found leisure
now and then to make himself useful. He served on the
Council, acted informally as consul for the men of Elis at
Athens, and lent the prestige of his international fame to
various embassies sent out to other cities. But his brother
was in Egypt commanding a warship in the fleet
the Athenians had sent to free that country from the
Persian. He was sailing up the broad Nile and would
never come down. One of Criton's cousins died in
Cyprus. Theocritos had perished in a second fleet with
which the Athenians had beaten the Corinthians and
their allies off the coasts of the Peloponnese. War with
Aegina broke out in the self-same year. It was Criton's
uncle, though fifty years of age, who died in that glorious
sea battle. His eldest nephew had been landed from that
fleet to besiege Aegina, as Criton himself had been
landed on Thasos very nearly ten years ago, which in

the onrushing sweep of history at Athens was two generations back.

In that extraordinary year when nearly every citizen between eighteen and fifty years old was serving abroad, Criton had not gone. Neither his district, which could have drafted him, nor he himself had thought it his duty. All were conscious that in order to win his third crown, he must waste not a moment. In the gymnasium he paraded his strength amid the lame and the old, or the very young.

Now the Corinthians, though beaten off the sea, made a final effort. Gathering their allies, they moved by land into the Megarid, calculating that by mastering Megara they would open a door through which they could at will march straight on Athens. Since the Athenians had no force left to send against them, they must either abandon the siege of Aegina or lose Megara; and they might just possibly by the gods' favor do both.

Thus thought the Corinthians, underestimating the invincible spirit of Athens. For, gathering together the youths over sixteen and the men over fifty, she sent them out against the army of Corinth. This time, towering over the half-grown boys in the ranks, Criton marched with them.

It was a grimly determined army, relying on spirit to take the place of strength. The young were exalted, the old resigned to die. Criton was neither. Perhaps he of all of them worried most about what he might lose. An unlucky spear-thrust might not be the end of him, but it would surely finish his chance at the games. He was not ready to be reduced, like Pancleon, to training others.

Though a motley group, they had a good commander who, perceiving that Megara would hold out if help were coming, had the sense to spare his men. They marched without undue haste and camped in the Megarid, while the Corinthians left Megara alone and came to meet them. The Athenians threw up no tents, having no baggage with them. Each bore five days' rations, and there was water nearby. The weather, as always at this time of year, was clear and dry. The veterans wrapped themselves in their cloaks and went to sleep, their shields and other equipment neatly beside them. A few of the boys did likewise. More sat and talked, too excited for fatigue. Criton would willingly have done the same, but he thought it better — being of course a marked man — to lie down and set an example. Half listening to what was said, half worrying over his own private thoughts, he dozed for a while.

Somebody giggled and woke him. For a moment he did not know where he was. Then he thought he was back again in those days of his military training with his friends. He lay there blinking and sorting these sensations out, while somebody said sharply:

"Psst! You'll wake the great man."

"That ox!" cried a high, disdainful voice. "He'd not stir if you kicked him."

"He won at Olympia," protested someone else, objecting more to the tone than to what had been said.

"There was a time," the scornful voice answered, "when men went to Olympia and won their crowns for the honor of the city. But in betweenwhiles, they found more to do for her than learning to jump an extra inch or run a bit faster. Nor would they give themselves insufferable airs over such silly achievements. I tell you, this thick-headed Criton might look all very well in Ithome or Melos, or some little spot where no one ever grows great. Here in Athens . . ."

"Oh, you again, Pisander," interrupted somebody laughing. "We all know you're going to outshine Pericles when it comes to your turn to lead the state. Go to sleep."

"If I'm going to die," Pisander retorted, "then I want to spend my last hours thinking over the glories that the rest of you may see. If, on the other hand, I live, why, then I want to remember the night before my first battle. You go to sleep."

Apparently the rest wished to, for nobody answered. Criton lay and stared at the stars. They were an age ahead of him now, these very young men. How simply had Hippias said, "I envy you, Criton!" Then Hippias had flung his own future away, as this Pisander might do. Was it through deaths such as these that the world had changed? At all events, if Criton won his third Olympic crown, he would see only the mocking smiles behind the cheering. In another five years, would the young men say his very statue was a piece of foolishness?

Would they take it down? Strangely enough, in spite of
the bitterness of these thoughts, Criton was not unhappy.
He merely had the feeling that he was glad to be fighting
next day in his first battle. If he survived it, he would
never feel easy in this new world, or yet in the old. His
future was not a very great thing to give the beloved city.
Let her make what she could of that and of his past.

In the year that Criton died to save the Megarid, the
ten tribes of Athens put up each a memorial stone
to those who had died for them in Cyprus and Egypt, in
Aegina and the Peloponnese, in the Aegean, in Boeotia,
and in the Megarid. They said nothing of Olympic victors or young men with a future. They wasted no words
on epitaphs, thinking such a list of efforts needed no further comment. In the midst of one of these lists there
came together the names of Pisander and Criton without
distinguishing how much each one had sacrificed or
whose gift was the greater.

# The Two Painters

## Athens About 470 B.C.

THE SHOP of Euphronios in the potters' quarter was smallish, dingy, and not remarkable for hustle or bustle. In a tiny room off the street a Scythian handyman was mixing clay in a trough in one corner. He used for the purpose a wooden paddle or his hands and was steeped to the elbows in brownish clay some three shades darker than the flaming, unkempt mass of his beard and hair. His working tunic, which he wore girt round the waist and pinned on one shoulder, had long ago taken on the

same indelible color. A lighter shade clung to his chest
and upper arms, so that in the half-light from the street
he might quite easily have passed for one of those unbaked terra-cottas which were stamped out of molds and
dried for the very cheapest of household gods or toys or
funeral trinkets.

"More clay, Xanthias," the potter muttered.

Xanthias scooped out a dollop of clay with his paddle
and brought it over. The potter twisted it between his
hands until it broke and regarded it glumly. "More
water, fool!"

Xanthias grunted, picked up the water pitcher, and
went off down the street to fill it at the fountain. The
potter slapped his two pieces together and twisted again.
He pinched off a bit and dropped it on the floor, which
was already brown with the trodden dust of earlier dis-
cards. He started the wheel with his foot and went on
kneading. Presently he threw the lump with hairbreadth
accuracy onto the center of his wheel. He dabbled his
hands in a basin of water and spun faster. Between his
fingers, the clay rose like a living thing. He mashed it
down and watched it rise again.

Someone strolled in from the street, bringing with him
into the damp, fusty air of the shop a strong smell of per-
fume. Even in the half-light, this was clearly an exquisite
young man, his woolen tunic white not with fuller's earth
but with glossy newness, his cloak depending from one
shoulder by a golden brooch and carefully weighted with
pellets at the corners. His dark hair, cropped fairly short

and naturally wavy, was arranged about his face in elaborate curls. His complexion, however, was brown, his figure athletic, and his manner, though assured, was not affected. He stood watching the potter, whose clay miraculously was taking on the shape of a wide, shallow bowl. It was not until the operation was complete enough for the potter to sheer off the lip with his knife that the young man spoke. "Well, Manes, did Euphronios paint me another?"

Manes nodded without looking up. He had stopped the wheel and was using a pair of lifters to set his bowl to dry on a shelf containing other similar bowls or narrow stems with rounded feet, all drying. He examined these, stooping until his nose almost touched the shelf. "Your cup's in the furnace." He spared a moment to gesture in the direction of the court, where Euphronios's furnace shared the open space with his hens, his household altar, and even to some extent with his womenfolk, who sometimes did their spinning in the small roofed colonnade on the north wall.

"Anything very special today?"

Manes shrugged a pair of bony shoulders. His fingers, flattened by his trade and almost double-jointed, were busy joining handles to a half-dried bowl. "He's only been drawing so far. He's still behind."

"He's always behind," remarked the young man with indignation. "Why anyone puts up with him, I don't know. Can't he train another artist?"

"Who wants another artist?" asked Manes sourly.

86 ATHENIANS OF THE GOLDEN AGE

"By Zeus, not I," the young man protested. "Yet Euphronios should train someone while he can. They say his eyes . . ."

"Eyes, bah!" retorted Manes rudely. "People gossip. The drawing's a strain for him, though. He's done so many designs and every one of them a masterpiece. Now mine, you see, are all the same." He took down a cup already fitted to its stem and spun it slowly, holding his scraper poised and staring moodily at the slight irregularities of the surface. With delicate precision, he applied the scraper for a moment, then took it away. Impatiently he raised his eyes and scowled at the waiting young man. "Come back tomorrow, Philip."

"You'll be opening your furnace soon," objected Philip. "Why should I not stay till you do. I'm tired of coming."

Manes merely narrowed his eyes as he turned to peer sharply at the dazzling sunlight framed by the street door. "That idle Xanthias!" He straightened his twisted frame to hobble over to his shelf. He took up a cup or two and inspected them, turning his back.

Philip shrugged and strolled into the inner court, where he looked at the furnace and peered at the two dampers, one for oxidizing the clay to orange-red, the other for blackening the pigment. He kicked carelessly at a hen, which fled squawking, and ogled a female figure, which retired out of sight in a hurry. Having thus exhausted the resources of the place, he turned to enter the room in which Euphronios did his painting.

This too was very small and rather gloomy. Euphronios needed a good light, to be sure, but he feared dust in his paint. Thus he and his assistant when at work chose sheltered corners, while the pigment was mixed in small amounts at a time and carefully covered. At the present moment, the assistant was at work on borders, partly using a stencil and a flexible ruler, partly drawing free-hand outlines with a fine brush and leaving the back-ground to be filled in later on with the paint, which in its unbaked state was merely a wash of the red-brown clay moistened with vinegar and mixed with potash. Eu-phronios himself was drawing on the inside of one of Manes's finished cups with a blunt instrument which made a little mark on the half-dried clay. His tired, red eyes were screwed up, and his forehead contracted into a desperate frown. As Philip entered, the artist muttered as though to himself, "Don't talk to me. Don't say any-thing at all. Just go away!"

"What's the matter with all of you today, Euphronios?" Philip demanded. "Here's your furnace cold, because I felt it — but Manes is in one of his moods and won't open it for me. As for you, I've waited thirty days; and you keep telling me it's done, or will be done. If I sail home without it, I'll not pay."

Euphronios dipped his finger in water and rubbed a line out. "Eh, what? Can't you see I'm busy drawing? Go away!"

"So I shall," retorted Philip. "And let me tell you, Eu-phronios, that you are not the only good vase painter in Athens. There's Meidias, for instance; and he's younger.

Everyone knows that you are by no means what you were."

The painter threw down his instrument with such force that it rolled away under his stool. "If fools would only let me work, I'd outshine Meidias as easily as all the rest; but you come in here . . ."

"Because you promised me a cup," the young man persisted. "A masterpiece from your own hand without a line on it from him," he nodded at the assistant. "None of your stencils and cheap borders. You promised it me to take back to Thessaly."

Euphronios tugged angrily at his beard as if it soothed his fingers to be doing something. "Is it my fault that Manes fired it wet and wasted my labor? It's drawn anew and even better. I fired it myself and ordered Manes not to lay a hand on it. If he'd dared open that furnace for you, I'd have sold him for what he would fetch to that fool, my neighbor."

Philip raised his well-marked brows. "I thought you informed me last time I was here that your neighbor had just died. You sounded pleased."

Euphronios cackled. "Oh, the old man died, the father. May Hades endure him. I couldn't. He made cheap pots."

"I should not have imagined his competition would have troubled you, then."

"No competition troubles me," Euphronios told him shortly. "I am Euphronios. But he gave the trade a bad name. And to make it worse, he was an Athenian."

Philip, who was already acquainted with the peculiar madness of Athenians about themselves and their city, did not pursue this. He shrugged his shoulders. "You're rid of him at least."

"Well, yes, in a way." Euphronios frowned. "He left a son, young Onesimos, who thinks he's a painter. They all do, even my lad in the corner here. It takes practice, not conceit, and also a talent which the gods give where they will. These boys might as easily aspire to be born king's sons; but they don't know it."

He grinned to himself, regarding his design with his head on one side. His right hand felt absently for his instrument; and Philip, perceiving that in another moment he would be forgotten, put in quickly, "Will you open the furnace for me, Euphronios? It's cold, as I just told you."

"Eh, what?" The painter seemed to have had an idea. "Just a moment." He bent down to grope on the floor.

"Will you open the furnace," Philip insisted, "or will you not? I warn you, if I go away once more, I'll go to Meidias, or even to young Onesimos, your neighbor."

"No such luck!" But Euphronios sat up. "You'll never leave me in peace, I know you well. All right, then. I'll open the furnace if I must and let you go." He rubbed his tired eyes and pushed back his stool to get up. He raised his voice to a shout. "You, Xanthias!"

"Master!" Xanthias appeared in the court, looking just as much clay-color in the sun as he had in the half-dark, except for his eyes, which blazed bright blue.

"The furnace, Xanthias!" Euphronios himself advanced into the court, closely followed by Philip, who did not omit to let his eyes wander in the direction of the colonnade on the north wall.

Xanthias was picking away with a pointed instrument at the furnace, which was beehive in shape and built of bricks plastered with clay to keep them in place. It was necessary for him to break a hole in the side to get at the oven, which was the easier for him to do because one portion of it had been sealed up with fresh clay which had cracked in drying and now flaked easily off. From behind this, Xanthias lifted out bricks, exposing ashes.

"Just rake off the oven," Euphronios ordered. "No one lays a hand on it today but myself. Then there's no stupid error."

Xanthias nodded. He had piled the loosened bricks to one side and was cleaning off the oven with a rake, transferring smears to himself and his garment till he looked like a half-finished black-figure painting. The oven itself was a great, pot-bellied piece of blackened earthenware with a heavy lid which it was not possible to lift without getting dirty. Euphronios, however, put Xanthias impatiently aside and without waiting for the ashes to be cleared out of his way, put his head in and got a grip on the rim with both hands. He heaved and emerged backwards, the lid coming with him.

"There you are," he said. "There . . ." He shut his mouth abruptly. A moment of absolute silence followed. Both Euphronios and Xanthias appeared completely frozen, the one clasping the blackened lid to himself, the other kneeling with one hand still outstretched and the rake in it.

"Let me have a look for myself." Philip put Euphronios aside and carefully inserted his head into the hole, holding back his spotless garments from contact with the edge. He blinked for a moment, unable to see anything after the brilliance of the sunlight in the court.

"Impossible!" muttered Euphronios behind his back. "I fired these myself, both with the green wood and the dry."

The oven swam slowly into focus, littered with fragments of cups, all of which had burst apart. Philip backed slowly and stood upright, shrugging his shoulders. "I see I must go to Meidias after all," he remarked. "A pity."

Euphronios came suddenly to life. He dropped the oven lid and pounced on Xanthias, seizing the rake out of his hand and starting to beat him about the head with the handle. "You did it, you villain! Confess!"

Xanthias put up his arms and twisted away from the blows. "I never laid hands on them, master. Nobody touched them but you. Nobody at all." He backed away out of range and then sought safety on the other side of the furnace. "May lightning from Zeus strike me dead if I touched one of them. May the gods of my own people drink my blood. May I shrivel and die!"

"It's witchcraft!" Manes had hobbled to the door of the shop and stood there blinking in the sun. "Someone put a curse on our furnace!"

"Man and boy," Euphronios retorted, "I've been firing that same furnace for fifty years. Don't tell me it's bewitched. I know my trade better than that. Those cups were wetted."

"I'd never do such a thing after thirty years of service," protested Manes nervously. "You know I wouldn't."

"And so it's Xanthias," Euphronios agreed. "Confess, you villain. I'll have you beaten till your bones are laid bare. I'll sell you to the silver mines and have you worked in chains. Admit you did it!"

"That's a very pretty girl indeed," remarked Philip suddenly, "now that I get a good view of her. She's trying to listen."

Euphronios swung round with a jerk. "Gorgo! How dare you? Exposing yourself in the court like any slave girl! Go up to your mother and tell her from me it's time that you were married. And don't shrug your shoulders at me. An older man like Eudoros is exactly what you need to keep you in order."

"She wanted to hear what went on," said Philip, whose comment had been inspired by curiosity, not bad manners. Little Gorgo had been peeping ever since they had started to open the furnace. In fact, she had been lurking in the colonnade when Philip first entered the court. Such interest in the circumstances seemed suspicious.

"Gorgo hears altogether too much!" shouted Euphronios, too angry to follow Philip's reasoning or put two and two together. "She sees too much as well. Her mother spoils her. She'll do what she's told for once, however. I'll deal with her mother, and Eudoros will look after her. He ought to beat her." This seemed to remind him of what he was about. "As for you, Xanthias . . ." he moved around the furnace, and Xanthias moved, too, keeping it between them.

"No, master! No, master!" Xanthias put up his hands in an imploring gesture. "I didn't touch them."

"Just wait until I touch you," Euphronios threatened.

They circled the furnace again. Philip, who had wasted his morning, and a number of other mornings also on Euphronios, decided that a cup from the master's hand was becoming more trouble than it was worth. He did not care whether Xanthias or Gorgo or Euphronios himself was really at fault. Even Philip's good nature was somewhat tired of dealing with an old man who grew more difficult every week. Thessalian aristocrats of Philip's circle were anxious to prove that they had a taste for culture. The name of Euphronios was known up there and had a standing which that of Meidias did not. But there might be something in discovering another painter and setting a fashion. Philip shrugged to himself and strolled off, leaving Euphronios swearing at a hen which had tripped him up, Xanthias protesting, and Manes adding his querulous voice to the clamor.

"Xanthias hasn't the brains to play such tricks," Manes was insisting sourly, "or the craft to carry them out. This was skillfully done."

Philip left them arguing and walked through the outer shop and into the street, where a young man rushed out of the next doorway to grab him by the arm.

"I have your c-cup," cried the young man anxiously. "Th-the cup you ordered from me. It is finished at last."

Philip stared at him, genuinely startled. This was a tallish, thinnish, stoop-shouldered young man in a working tunic which was spattered untidily with clay and pot-ash. His manner was nervous, and his fingers positively trembled on Philip's arm.

"I ordered no cup from you," Philip said coldly, releasing himself. The familiarity of tradesmen and even slaves in this town was not very easy to become accustomed to. Though Philip was a tolerant, good-natured man as a rule, he felt annoyed.

The young man dodged in front of him to prevent him from moving off. "Y-your slave came into my shop ten days ago and ordered . . . I was w-waiting for you to fetch it. That is, you are Philip, are you not? I p-promise you will like it. It is the best thing I ever painted."

"And who," demanded Philip, looking him up and down, "are you? And what reputation have you as a painter that I should seek you out?"

"Why, I am Onesimos, sir," retorted the young man, assuming an injured air. "Surely you remember. A-and so far I have not painted much. My father, you see, was a potter; and our artists were all slaves. We made cheap pots. But now that I am my own master, your slave coming to us was the greatest piece of luck that ever befell me. Only let me show you . . ."

Philip stared at him in silence for a moment. His wits

were at work putting two and two together. He certainly had not entrusted his slave with any such commis-
sion or even sent him off to the shop of Euphronios on
any errand. Besides, this young Onesimos was nothing
of an actor. His stammer and his nervousness gave him
away. The whole thing was a fraud.

"People told me I should find the ways of your democracy strange," said Philip reflectively. "And I must say
I do. For I should have thought there was work for all
without your conspiring to ruin another man's trade,
and he a painter renowned throughout all Greece."

Onesimos went scarlet, but he put up a fight. "If you
mean old Euphronios, why, he's a tyrant so crabbed that
there's no bearing with him. We've been neighbors all
our lives, yet when my father asked him if I might enter
his workshop as an apprentice, he said . . ."

"I don't want to know what he said," cried Philip,
really impatient. "Are the dealings of you petty tradesmen my affair?"

"N-no, of course not, sir," agreed Onesimos, suddenly
humble. "But my cup — your cup — I have it here inside."

Philip hesitated and was lost. Onesimos almost tugged
him inside his shop, which was larger and cleaner than
that of Euphronios and more active. Three potters were
at work, while other slaves fetched and carried, swept,
mixed, set pots to dry. The room for the painting,
which was visible through an open door, seemed nearly
as busy. Onesimos, however, led the way into his court,

where the furnaces had been opened and finished pots of
all sizes and shapes were stacked under a canopy. Philip
looked around him. No hens and no altar seemed to in-
dicate that this little yard served nothing but the workshop. Across it rose the house, no doubt with an entrance onto some other street and a yard of its own. The
women's quarters in the upper floor had windows looking in this direction. The lower floor was blank, except
for a door.

"This way," Onesimos said, following the direction of
Philip's glance uneasily. He tugged at Philip's cloak.

Philip disengaged himself. It happened that his eye-
sight was exceptionally keen. Besides, he saw no reason
to consider the embarrassment of Onesimos, to whom
presumably he owed the destruction of a vase by the master painter.

"Gorgo visits your sister, I perceive," he remarked with
malice. "Or is it your wife?"

Onesimos blushed and stammered again. "M-my
mother." He appeared to think he ought to explain and
hastily added, "There is a way across the roofs, and ever
since Gorgo was little, she has been much with us. You
see, Euphronios does not like her in his own court, which
is not private. B-but you will not concern yourself with
our affairs, as you just said."

"Naturally not," agreed Philip calmly. "Besides, I
imagine Gorgo is merely telling your mother that Euphronios means to make her marry. To be sure, you may

miss her after such long intimacy, especially as Euphronios has been so careless about it."

He had succeeded in silencing the young man and making him angry. Onesimos glared at him with an expression which a tradesman would only dare to assume in the city of Athens, where vulgar folk gave themselves airs. Philip promised himself that if the wretched fellow attacked him, he would break his skinny neck. But he was not forced to these extremes. Onesimos turned sullenly away, picked up a cup, and thrust it into his hand. "Well, there it is."

Philip glanced at it and felt surprise. The circular painting on the nearly flat inside was a portrait of Philip, recognizable enough with his regular features and formally arranged hair. He had taken up a shield, which partly concealed him and by its round shape emphasized the design. With this on his left arm, he was bending forward to pick up a helmet, so that the curve of his body fitted naturally into the circular frame. The perfect gracefulness of this quite simple design had led the painter to idealize Philip's squarish figure, making him slenderer and younger than he was. The drawing was not signed, but round the edge of it was written: Philippos Kalos, Philip the Fair.

Philip looked at this a long time, studying the simple perfection of its lines and revising his opinion of young Onesimos. He had talent of no common kind, and old Euphronios had been a fool to have missed it. He should

have taken this young man into his studio and bound
him to himself by marrying him to Gorgo. It was an artist's business to see something more in Onesimos than
nervousness and a shambling figure. Probably Euphronios had never so much as glanced at what the young
man had painted.

"Can you paint any more to match this?" he demanded abruptly.

Onesimos fidgeted, with that same gesture that Euphronios had of playing with his chin. He, too, must be
doing something with his long, nervous hands. "I'm not
quite certain. The back is not as good."

Philip turned the cup over. There on the outer side

was a pair of pictures. Philip, dressed for a journey and with a wide hat on his head, was taking leave of his father. Behind him stood his horse, head bent to nuzzle at his arm. On the other side of the cup he was coming back from hunting, dog at heels and game dangling from a spear across his shoulder. Neither had the distinction which Euphronios would have given such a subject. But the circular design was the work of a master. He turned the cup over to study it again. Great art was needed in the firing of such designs, for the clay surface must first be oxidized red, then blackened all over by the use of green wood and the adjustment of dampers. Then finally it must be oxidized again just sufficiently to turn the unpainted figure red, leaving the black glaze on the background and the fine lines of the drawing. Even the slightest mistake in one of these processes might result in a blurring; and it often did so. But this cup was perfect.

"How much do you want for it?" Philip inquired. He intended to have it, but the work of an unknown youngster ought to be cheap.

Onesimos fumbled with his chin again. "I-I chiefly want you to show it to Euphronios. He-he won't even look at my work. So we thought, that is, I thought . . ."

"And Gorgo thought," prompted Philip, almost laughing. The girl still peeped from the window, spying on them for a few seconds at a time, then drawing away.

"Yes, well, and Gorgo thought . . ." Onesimos swallowed, "that her grandfather would be curious about a cup which had been made for you, sir. It is not signed, as you see — nothing to annoy him before he takes in the design."

"Euphronios is so mad with anger now," Philip reminded him, "that I hardly suppose he will look at anything. If you really wanted to work under him, I could imagine better methods of making yourself agreeable than breaking his cups."

"But we didn't!" Onesimos exclaimed. He glanced up hastily at the window and added, "That is, we didn't mean to. W-we planned to be ready before Euphronios was. He's always behind. B-but then I could not satisfy myself with the design. I worked at it these thirty days — I need experience. So Gorgo said she would delay the firing somehow. That's all she meant to do, I promise you."

Philip caught another glimpse of Gorgo at the window. She was certainly pretty, but it did cross his mind that he would rather not be her grandfather or husband. He did not think either of them would ever be her master. Indeed, if Philip could have condescended to interest himself in tradesmen's affairs, he might just possibly have given this young man a warning. But what was it to him whether Onesimos were fated to be henpecked or no? "I wonder," he remarked aloud, "if all the women-folk whom you Athenians keep so carefully secluded must have their own way. In Thessaly, our customs are a trifle freer, and there is give and take. This would seem to me wiser."

Onesimos appeared not to interest himself in these random thoughts. "If you will but show this to Euphronios," he persisted, "why, then Gorgo can smooth his anger down. She manages him."

"I do not doubt she does," replied Philip politely. "I shall certainly show him your cup, and I wish you a happy life with him and Gorgo."

"I thank you," replied the young man, surprised, "for your condescension . . . Euphronios," he added after a moment's thought, "is an Athenian, not one of that alien gang. And so am I. We shall get on."

It was Philip's turn to be surprised. "All mad in the same way! Perhaps you will."

# The Day He Was Athens

## Athens 454 B.C.

"He's a good provider," Phano remarked. She threw the spindle out in front of her with an expert twirl, let the thread twist for just the right amount of time, then jerked to bring it back to her hand, rolling up the thread as it came. She pulled out more wool from the distaff, adding thoughtfully, "Some aren't."

"Don't I know it," Melissa agreed. "Poor Isthmias!" She reached for one of the little honey cakes and bit into it. "Excellent! My dear, your girl's a treasure."

"Isthmias is fond of her man, or so they say."

"More fool she."

"Well, I don't know." Phano threw the spindle again. She watched it come back to her hand. "At least he doesn't beat her."

"That poor Plangon with her two black eyes!" Melissa shook her head. "I'll tell you something, Phano. Marriage is a lottery, that's what it is. A lottery."

Phano nodded, much struck by the comparison. "You're right, Melissa. And you drew a white one."

Melissa helped herself again. "I really oughtn't, but just this once. Yes, dear, he's easygoing. 'Go out and order yourself a pair of shoes,' he says. Then if I pop in to see you instead of coming straight home, it's all one to him. He has his dinner on time when he dines in, which isn't often. And as long as he's comfortable, he doesn't grumble."

"Well, Leon never grumbles either exactly. Only he doesn't like my gadding about, you see, Melissa."

"Gadding about!" Melissa lifted indignant hands. "I haven't seen you outside your own house since the festival of the Thesmophoria. That was six months back. You don't visit anyone. And when I looked for you at the Dionysia in the theater two months ago, you just weren't there."

"That was the time little Conon had a fever. You'd hardly think it to look at him now." Phano smiled at her son, who was dragging his two-wheeled cart full of stones round the yard, shouting 'gee-up!' to himself and pawing the ground like a horse. "I thought we might lose him, I really did. We were frantic, Leon and I."

"It didn't keep Leon from the theater," snorted Melissa.

Phano smiled and shrugged this off. "Oh well, a man!"

"I daresay, Phano. But you're just making excuses.

The truth is, you're too easy, and Leon trades on your good nature. Nag him a little."

Phano's round face looked distressed. She had been five years married and was barely twenty yet. Leon was thirty-five. It was always easier to do what Leon expected. "I wonder how Leon would like it if I nagged him," she timidly inquired.

"Like it? He's not meant to like it. And don't make him comfortable unless he's reasonable, dear. None of these delicious cakes, for instance . . . I must have another."

"I really don't think I dare nag Leon," Phano remarked.

Melissa looked at her indignantly, but seeming to realize that she must make the best of poor material, she countered briskly, "Question him, then."

"Question him? What about?"

"About what he does, of course. That's always the first step. If you know half the things he does himself, he's bound to let you have a little more freedom. I'll wager Leon never tells you anything. Did he tell you, for instance, that he's a candidate for the Council next year, and the drawing's today?"

Phano's hands actually stopped their rhythmic motions for a moment. "No! He never did. Are you sure, Melissa?"

"My Gylon's a candidate, too," Melissa said. "For the second time. The tribe put him up last year, but he had no luck with the drawing."

"The Council!"

"I tell you one thing, Phano," Melissa urged. "If Leon gets in, you make him give you a few ornaments. You're getting shabby. Besides, a man's only on the Council twice in life. He'll be excited. That's the time to look after yourself."

"The Council! Well I never!"

"He may not have luck with the lot."

"Leon always has luck when it comes to drawing lots," said Phano calmly.

"All the better for you." Melissa shook her finger. "You remember . . . a new brooch and ribbons at the very least. It's the Panathenaea next month. You'll be in the procession, I shouldn't wonder."

"Oh, no!"

"Why not, then, Phano? You're decently born, and though Leon does work at the cabinetmaking himself, still, if he's on the Council . . ."

"I couldn't expect it."

"Just one more, and then I must go." Melissa took the last of the little cakes and was actually holding it to her mouth when Phano gave a startled cry. "Great Mother Demeter! Leon's come home early."

Melissa got up in a hurry, hiding the little cake under her cloak. "Where's my girl? Never here when she's wanted. Wasting her time gossiping with your girl! Thratta! Thratta! Now remember what I say . . . a brooch and ribbons. You need a new dress, dear. And you stand up for yourself. You ought to be able to put your nose out of doors now and then. We all need a change."

Thratta came running. Melissa scolded her and bustled her out of the alcove off the court where the ladies were sitting. Leon, meanwhile, had halted beside the altar of Zeus, politely unwilling to notice another man's wife, yet not refraining from conveying displeasure to Phano by his expression. Leon was a very little man, a decent tradesman and a conscientious husband, but not fitted to make much of an impression on people at large. He was not wealthy enough to be asked to train a chorus, outfit a ship, produce a play, or perform any of the other services by which men made themselves important to their city. He was not clever enough to be a social success, had never happened to have been chosen by lot for any office. On military service or in the exercise ground, his size was against him. Actually Phano was the only human being who looked up to him with any reverence or awe, and his strictness with her was not unkindly meant. It merely gave him satisfaction to assert himself with someone.

"That woman again!" he said to Melissa's retreating back. "I thought I told you I did not wish you to waste your time in idle gossip."

Phano's eyes filled with tears. "She — she comes here, Leon, and I don't like to send her away. I did try to go on with my spinning, b-but she ate all the c-cakes w-we made for dessert!"

Leon, who had a sweet tooth, frowned at this. But he was not a badhearted man, and he could not help seeing that the visit was not Phano's fault. Besides, he was full of good news and wanted to be cheerful. He patted Phano. "I'm sure you did all that you should. It's just that I don't like the woman. I expect you don't either."

"Oh, no," agreed Phano, readily convinced. "But you see, I've always known her."

"Never mind her," said Leon, impatient for congratulations. "You'll never imagine what it is I've been doing today."

"Oh, Leon!" cried Phano, too excited for discretion. "You've done it then! I knew you would have luck. You're on the Council!"

Leon, the wind completely taken out of his sails, frowned again. "There you are, you see. I knew that woman gossiped."

"And your new cloak not ready to send to the fuller for bleaching," babbled Phano. "We might wash the old one perhaps . . . but your tunic! Oh, Leon! How important you will be! Think of Conon with his father on the Council!"

"He won't know what it all means yet." Leon smiled at his son, who was trying to fit the pebbles from his cart into the mouth of a little jar.

"He will soon. He's getting so big. Do you think we ought to crown him with a garland for the Anthesteria this year? He's really old enough."

"Time enough to see when winter comes. But now, about the Council . . ."

"Oh yes, the Council. Now you must, yes, you really must, Leon, tell me all about everything. I want to know."

Leon allowed himself to be led into the alcove and to sit in Melissa's seat. Melissa had been quite wrong in fact when she supposed that Leon did not confide in his wife. But since most of his triumphs had hitherto been in his workshop and most of his failures in public or social life, it was only natural that most of what he said had concerned his business. It was with his business that he started today . . . how when the officials of the tribe had approached him to be a candidate for Council and had made such a point of it, he had considered that with the workshop doing so well and the slave foreman properly trained, as he now was, it might be possible for Leon to free himself for public life. He had felt himself fitted for some while to do such a thing, but the opportunity and the time had not been ripe.

"No, indeed." Phano's education and her experience might be small, but Leon's business was as familiar to her as her household. She followed it keenly, knew all the slaves by name, though she seldom saw them, and could recite the orders Leon received as well as he. "Why, even last year when old Cerdon died and you bought two new slaves, it would not have been prudent."

"Just so." Leon was relaxing and expanding. He could count upon Phano to agree with whatever he said, and really her comments seemed quite intelligent to him, considering her sex.

"Why, even Pericles and the generals don't really *govern* the city, not the way the Council does," pursued Phano happily.

This was too much even for Leon. He perceived that Phano's political education was fragmentary, and he proceeded in his systematic way to give her a lecture. But what with his desire to magnify the importance of the Council and what with Phano's eagerness to exaggerate what he said, he made no progress.

"Well, if the Assembly can't so much as discuss any measure till it's been passed by the Council, even Pericles has to go first to you, doesn't he?"

"Well, yes."

"And now that you're on the Council, you could, Leon, propose anything you liked as well as he."

Leon thought there might be a slight difference in fact, but he did not say so.

"And the monies of the state are in your hands, oh, and the examination of all those accounts, and the fleet, and the cavalry, and the public buildings, and the festivals. It's the Panathenaea in the New Year," said Phano, thinking wistfully for a moment of Melissa's words about the procession. "You'll be so important!"

Leon smiled indulgently. He had his qualms, and Phano's enthusiasm was exactly what he needed. "Don't forget," he reminded her gaily, "after all, I'll be one of five hundred."

"Five hundred!" Phano's tone made little of this figure. "Besides, for a tenth of the year, there's the Standing Committee. You'll be one of fifty then."

"And if I have luck with the drawing of lots," Leon pointed out, "mind you, only if I have luck, I might be President for a night and a day."

"You will have luck, I feel sure of it. To be the President! Why, that's like . . . being Athens!"

Leon laughed and told her she was foolish, but all the same next day he bought her a ribbon. He bought her a brooch when he passed the scrutiny of the outgoing council, proving to them that he was of free-born descent, was not a state debtor, had honored his father, and looked after his family tombs. He even said nothing when Melissa popped in once more to say that Gylon had been a lucky man, too, and that her nephew would escort herself and Phano as well to the Panathenaea.

"You can't expect the men to think of us, dear," Melissa explained. "Why, Gylon's puffed up like a bullfrog with his own importance! Thinks himself Pericles, I wouldn't wonder. As for the detail of how I'm to watch the festival without him, he can't be bothered with that. Your Leon's no better."

Actually Leon for once was grateful to Melissa for solving a tiresome small problem. Besides, he was indulgent towards Phano, partly because she had entered into his feelings with perfect sympathy, and partly because his importance for the moment did not require to be asserted. He would be walking in the procession himself, watching the games and the contests from his special seat of honor. Indeed, if his tribe won the very first month as the Standing Committee, he would in effect be presiding on the occasion. The prospect affected him with nervous awe. This gorgeous festival, occurring only every four years, had become the celebration and the symbol in recent times of Athenian greatness. All the members of the Athenian League sent delegates. The procession conveying her new and glorious robe to the image of Athene was made up of the noblest and fairest that the city of Athens could find. In such company Leon would walk. He might even be President on that particular day, though he trembled at the notion.

Leon need not have troubled himself with such dreams. The Panathenaea came with the New Year in July. His turn on the Standing Committee was fixed for the following June, at the end of the year when most of the business and all the great festivals were safely past. In the meanwhile, though the Council met most days, Leon discovered that one man amid five hundred is not as important as he may think he will be when he is chosen.

Councils selected by lot from the citizen body might be imagined to be year after year much the same. Somehow or other, this was never the case at Athens. There always proved to be a core of people who set the tone. The Council of Leon's year was dominated by a clique of thrusting, expansionist merchantmen who were at the same time ready to support Pericles in a bid for power within Greece, while backing his opponents in vigorously pursuing the war against Persia. In this year, therefore, the Athenians sent a squadron of fifty ships to reinforce the expedition which they had already dispatched to assist the Egyptians in their revolt against Persia. Next, having but few warships left at home, they scraped up an army to restore the king of Thessaly, who was personally friendly to Athenian power. Such measures, though decreed by the Assembly, were debated hotly in Council first. Leon listened. He voted. He even discussed his opinion in private with Phano as though it mattered. Men like Gylon, however — who was head and shoulders taller than Leon and with a bull-like voice — found it easy to assert themselves amid the petty hucksters and farmers who made up the Council's bulk. Leon could not do so. He was never selected for one of the administrative committees. He was never near the center of those informal groups which met between sessions and thrashed out business. On the rare occasions when he voiced an opinion, he could not deceive himself into thinking it had any weight.

The year which Leon had entered with such high hopes was turning out unsatisfactorily. Even his business was not going quite as well as it ought, for lack of attention. Frustrated in every other way, Leon asserted himself at home to the point of forbidding Melissa to enter his house with her talk about Gylon and how he with his cronies ran the Council. It was an unworthy revenge on fate, but he had no other.

Summer had worn into winter and winter to spring. The dramatic performances of the Dionysia in March brought about another meeting between Melissa and Phano. "You look pale," Melissa said, "and no wonder. Leon's a failure, that's what he is; and he takes it out on you."

"He's on the next Standing Committee but one," said Phano stoutly.

Melissa snorted. "Well, he has to be on it some time, doesn't he? Lucky it'll be a quiet month, if you ask me. Gylon's President in three days when the comedies are played. I wish women could see them."

"Leon will be President in time," Phano assured her.

"Don't count your lot before it is drawn," retorted Melissa. "Fourteen of them draw a blank, and Leon's as likely to do so as not. Best thing if he should. Gylon says he's utterly feeble. Why, the tribe would never have asked him to stand, Gylon says, if there weren't so many men away in Egypt."

"Don't talk to me about Leon like that," said Phano and burst into tears.

"Well, he forbade me the house, didn't he?" But Melissa felt a little ashamed of herself. "There, Phano! You know how I run on. I didn't mean it. Besides, you can't cry here. They're coming on the stage!"

Phano wiped her eyes with the corner of her cloak, but though the prologue of the tragedy began, her tears kept flowing quietly. Truth was, she felt dragged down by the long winter, which had been an anxious one. Conon was rising four and spoiled. He was having tantrums. Both Leon and Phano wanted another baby, and the delay in its coming was a disappointment. As for the excitement of Leon's being on the Council, that very soon faded away. He never told her what went on, but said she would not understand. She had understood perfectly when he talked about his business, but even that subject now was apt to annoy him. Leon was fretful, and he seemed to find fault more often than he used to. As the tragedy unfolded on the stage, Phano's tears dried up in sheer excitement, but when the moment came to weep for the death of the hero, she found it natural to let them flow again so profusely that Melissa rebuked her.

"You're making a spectacle of yourself, dear. It's only a play."

"I don't really think I feel very well."

"It must be the sun," said Melissa with alarm. "The first warm day of spring. Have something to drink, dear."

Phano accepted the pitcher of water and wine very meekly. There were two more tragedies to sit through, and in fact she was longing to see them. The brilliant costumes, the painted masks, the music and dancing, the poetry, the very crowd of spectators in the theater made such a contrast to her quiet domestic life that every minute was charged with almost unbearable excitement. In spite of the lowness of her spirits, home and Leon had already faded into a vague background where they did not for the moment greatly matter. She sat through the rest of the morning dreaming of the loves and deaths of long-dead heroes, and she was too rapt to cry again. When Melissa challenged her at the end to declare which play was best, she could only sigh contentedly as she came out of her daze and answer, "I'll ask Leon."

"Don't you ever make up your own mind?" Melissa snorted.

"Not where Leon knows best," replied Phano simply. The stir and the tragedy onstage had left her feeling as calm as after a good cry. "Of course he tells me what I should think about important things because he's a man."

Perhaps Leon too had been lifted above petty troubles, because he not only obligingly told Phano what to think, but praised her cooking and remarked that old Lydia was all very well as a baby's nurse, but that Conon was getting beyond her and he would have to see about proper help. This was all the more generous of Leon because he really was worried about the effect on his business of his being on the Standing Committee for over a month. The Council already took a fair proportion of his time. The Standing Committee would take it all and force him frequently to sleep in the Round House at night, where the holy fire of the city was never allowed to go out. He would have to neglect the shop for days on end. No doubt about it, a foreman, however well trained, does not equal the master.

Phano was fussing about the Standing Committee, too. She had Leon's new cloak fresh-washed and had been weaving a tunic for him as well, which was just ready.

She had needed a dress for herself, but that could easily wait till the end of the year, when if old Lydia were to have more time on her hands, she could help with the spinning. When it came Leon's turn to be President, he must look handsome.

Leon wished she would not talk in this way, but he did not like to tell her so. His year had gone badly, and he had lost confidence in his luck. The Standing Committee had thirty-six days, and there were fifty people in it. Almost a third of them would draw a blank.

They held the drawing on their first day as a Standing Committee. One of the pushing sort was quickly chosen to stand by an urn and draw out names in the order in which they should preside. There was a mild tension over the little group. Not everybody thought much of the office, which was indeed without power. Still, there was dignity in being head of state, in keeping the Seal, the keys of the treasury and archives, in presiding over Council and Assembly. There were four Assemblies this month in the regular way, and only two festivals, neither important. The business of the year was practically over, and much of the time of the Council would be spent in examining incoming officials, a simple routine. There were, in other words, no particular prizes of special days to be won. It would be, as Melissa had said, a quiet month.

There was, Leon told himself, no real reason why any sensible man should covet this office. He would have to be on hand for twenty-four hours, and there would be little to be done. All the same, he felt some satisfaction in hearing his name called out for the twentieth day, a perfectly blank one as far as he could tell. It happened, however, that two ships were already at sea, one to the east of him and one to the west, which would put in on the twentieth day and make it eventful.

The first of these came into the port of Piraeus in the gray before dawn at a moment when Leon, who had taken over the keys the previous night, was asleep in the Round House with his best cloak carefully folded over the Seal, while a third of the Committee snored beside him. There was nothing remarkable about this boat, which was a simple, round-bellied trading ship with twenty oars, not even Athenian. It hailed from Lemnos and had been puttering around the eastern seas since early March, buying, selling, or swapping. It knew its way about the Piraeus and did not bother with the western shore, where the slips and arsenals for the war fleet were very nearly empty. Making for the eastern side where the porticoes were and the warehouses for the reception of goods, it started to nose its way between an Athenian loading up with jars of oil for the Black Sea and a Syracusan discharging a cargo of hides, which unfortunately stank.

"Hey you!" cried a voice from the latter. "Look out with your oars!"

It might be imagined that the crew of a battered old

trading ship would have been handier. The Piraeus, however, was very crowded just now; and besides, the Lemnian had worked his rowers all night, having come on a cargo of rare woods which the skillful craftsmen of Athens would be hungering for if he could only outdistance his rivals in the same trade. At all events, an oar of the newcomer's caught one of the steering poles of the Syracusan, which was trailing in the water. There was a crack.

"You lubberly sons of jackasses, you!" called the Syracusan angrily. "Can't you so much as draw up to a wharf without smashing into someone else? Think you own the Piraeus?"

"Trailing your steering oar!" retorted the Lemnian master, climbing on the poop ready to throw his rope around a bollard. "You lazy apes, you filthy, stinking hawkers of carrion. Didn't anyone ever warn you to take that in? Serve you right if we smashed it."

The Syracusan retorted by an unflattering account of the Lemnian's ancestry, which he saw fit to describe in vivid detail. The Athenian and other ships in earshot, awakened by the din, perceived that it was dawn and that their masters, supercargoes, owners of consignments, or purchasers of goods would soon be gathering from their billets in the town. They joined with alacrity in the slanging match which was already going on, by no means confining their repartees to one side or the other. The shouting ran up and down the wharfs, while the

Lemnian owner of the incoming ship jumped ashore without ever running the usual gantlet of questions. He was not sorry, for he had foreseen delay, though he had no news.

It was still very early in the morning, but there was much to be done. The usual procedure, after paying the proper harbor dues, was to land a sample of goods for display in the public porticoes or warehouses established for that business. Much, however, depended on showing one's wares to the right people. The Lemnian master could safely leave the ship and the unloading to his second-in-command, but the all-important question of selling he handled himself. Cutting, therefore, around the porticoes, which were just beginning to fill up, he dodged down an alley where the barbers plied their trade and purveyed news.

Ships being what they were, it stood to reason that a mariner coming ashore would need a trim. Barbering, moreover, was a leisurely trade which left energy for gossip. Thus the barbershops of the Piraeus had become little clubs where people waiting for a haircut or a shave were joined by those who wanted business. A clever barber knew everything that went on in town: who was rich, who was poor, whose credit was shaky, the state of the market for onions or fish, and even the prospect of getting a good price for something special like a cargo of rare woods express from Cyprus. Whatever you wanted, the barber could pass you on to someone useful.

He would not, however, do any such thing before he had trimmed you and picked you clean of news. The barber was never in a hurry.

With these considerations in mind, the Lemnian entered the shop he usually went to, which was an alcove overflowing into the street and at present occupied by the barber himself, a man whom he was shaving, a slave tending water pots and sweeping hair, and two early loungers. These latter said good day, as did the barber, though for the moment without looking round. As for the victim of the shave, he kept his mouth shut. The barber had him by the ear and was sawing at his cheek. A straight razor is a ticklish instrument when used with cold water and without any soap. Nobody expected him to move a muscle or speak, and he did not do so.

"You in last night?" asked one of the lounging men. "You're early stirring."

" 'Smorning," said the Lemnian briefly, moving over to lean against the wall. "Got a valuable cargo."

"Where from?"

The Lemnian hesitated. "Well, actually Cyprus, but I've no news at all. That Samian who got in here yesterday told me all I know. In fact, we left together."

"Ah, well. All quiet in Cyprus?"

"If you can call it quiet," the Lemnian said. "Of course they're worried about what the Persian will do."

The barber, razor poised, turned briefly around to say, "The Cyprians never trusted us Athenians. We'll show them when we win in Egypt."

The Lemnian sucked in his breath and let it out with a little gasp. "I'd not have believed it, though I always said you were an extraordinary people."

"Not have believed what?" The barber transferred his grip to his victim's nose and advanced his razor, smiling a little. He was used to the notion that foreigners marveled at the Athenians, but he still liked to be told so.

"You ask what?" repeated the Lemnian. "Why, that you could ever have taken so great a disaster so calmly. Two hundred and fifty ships. Fifty thousand men. All lost, and you merely say 'when we win in Egypt.'"

"Fifty thou . . ." With a sudden start, the barber had sliced a great gash in his victim's cheek, so deep that the flesh gaped open and the blood began to pour down his neck and over his tunic. The barber neither let go the nose nor reached for cobwebs. He seemed to stand frozen, while the victim himself neither moved nor spoke. The blood dripped on the floor.

"All *lost,* did you say?" The barber had a queer little whispering voice as though there were something stuck in his throat. "Did you say *lost?*" His color was a strange whitish-green and there were tears in his eyes. He took his hand away from the other man's face and stood up, shaking his head. "You've heard some rumor. A rumor, that's what it is. They can't be . . . *lost.*" He fixed imploring eyes on the Lemnian, who had gone almost as white.

"But the Samian, the warship!" cried the Lemnian loudly. "There were six ships which turned and fled, he said, and escaped with their lives. All the rest of these went down the African coast, but this one Samian came into Cyprus with the news. He left there the morning I did so, and with two hundred oars. Two hundred oars! Where is he?"

"A Samian," said the barber with a groan. "He went to Samos, no doubt, leaving us Athenians to be told by some chance comer looking for a . . . barber."

This was too true to be disputed. The Samians were almost the only ally which still sent a contingent to fight beside the Athenians instead of supplying their war chest with money. No doubt this Samian ought to have reported to Athens, but probably he had not dared after running away. The barber had dropped his razor and buried his face in his hands. The injured man put his fingers to his face, looked at the blood, and started to mop himself, while the slave came over with water in a basin and with cobwebs. "Oh, my son!" muttered one of the loungers to himself. "Oh, my son Diodotos, my only son!"

The Lemnian, who had forgotten the two loungers, glanced around. Only the one was still there. The other had already slipped out down the street with the tidings. In the distance, a woman began to keen on a shrill, mourning note. The barber took his head from his hands and pulled himself together.

"This is news for the Council," he said. "You saw that Samian and his crew. You spoke with them, I have no doubt. If you stay here even a few minutes more, you'll be mobbed. Come on! We're going to Athens."

"But my cargo!" The Lemnian protested. "I've got a cargo of . . ."

"Fool!" cried the barber. "D'you think there'll be buying and selling in the port on a day like this? Fifty thousand! There's not a man, be he Athenian born or foreign either, but has a relative or a dear friend gone to Egypt. Two hundred and fifty ships, man! The dockyard's empty, or nearly so, as you must have seen for yourself. I say, come on!"

It is more than an hour's walk from the Piraeus to Athens, even when men are in a special hurry. Besides, the barber, as one who dealt in favors, could not help stopping on the road to unburden the news to a few special clients. Thus by the time the Lemnian arrived, Leon was already preparing to preside at one of the regular meetings of the Council. Everything at once was thrown into a turmoil. Slaves went scurrying to call the Standing Committee together early. Some members of the Council came in at once, for rumor was spreading in Athens with the swiftness of a sudden plague. Questioned, the Lemnian left no room for any hope. The original expedition had been blockaded on an island in the Nile, where its situation, though awkward, had not seemed desperate to Athens. The Persian, however, had succeeded in draining one channel and crossing dry-shod with a vast army. He had put the Greeks to the sword. Thereafter, the relief expedition, sailing just too late into the Nile, had been attacked from the land side by the victorious Persians and from seaward by three hundred Phoenician ships which they also had with them. Only this Samian and a very few others had escaped. It was utter disaster.

Such were the tidings which met the anxious Councilors as they came hurrying together. They were not statesmen; and in face of a crisis so unexpected, they felt panic. If the expedition to Thessaly had not been undertaken as well . . . If they had not decided to throw more ships and men away in Egypt . . . If they had not waited till this spring when it was too late . . . If the people had never been deluded into the Egyptian adventure at all . . . Even Gylon and his loud-mouthed friends had lost their heads and were blaming one another. Others simply wrung their hands. Three hundred Phoenician ships on the sea, and no fleet ready! Many were struggling with the shock of private grief and spoke at random.

Leon let them talk, or rather clamor. His own feelings were as confused as theirs, but reponsibility weighed on him more. Things ought to be done. Since, however, his Standing Committee was of no use in maintaining order, Leon had no alternative but to wait while shaping something desperate in his mind which he wanted to say.

Leon saw his chance at last and got up, gesturing for silence. He obtained a sudden hush. The Council was anxious to have someone tell it what to do. Men looked and listened.

"We must get a fleet on the sea." Leon had forgotten the arts of public speaking altogether. "Ships cost money." He heard himself speaking into a silence which made his voice sound strange in his own ears. "I am not a rich man, but I will sell half what I have and give it to the state."

He sat down, his hands trembling. He and Phano would struggle through some lean years, but this did not matter. He was convinced in his own mind. The rest of the Council might do what it would. For a moment, its silence was as great as its former clamor had been. No one spoke.

"I will outfit a ship at my own cost," cried Gylon suddenly.

"And I."

"And I."

There was an outcry as all of them like sheep followed their leader.

"Here is Pericles," called someone. "He desires the President's permission to speak to the Council."

Leon roused himself to reply, "He has it."

The eyes of the Councilors followed Pericles dubiously as he walked forward. This expedition to Egypt had been none of his making. They knew it, and all expected him to reproach them for their folly.

"This is no moment for casting blame." Pericles also was taking his cue from Leon. He was abrupt, and the devices by which he played on the hearts of men were conspicuously absent. "There will be a time for blame and a time for mourning later. I will make up Leon's gift to the cost of outfitting one ship, since he is a brave man who has set us all an example. In my own name, I will outfit a second ship. However, there are things to be done before this. Send the heralds through the city to call the Assembly together. Only the people can vote us a fleet. Only they can pass a measure to remove the Treasury of our League from the island of Delos, where it lies exposed to a raid. We must bring it to Athens."

He sat down, and there was a hum. The treasury of the allied Greeks for the war against Persia had been located at Delos for the express purpose of preventing the Athenians from controlling it completely. If it were transferred, the contributions of the other allies would become something very like tribute. All saw this, for the use of these funds was often in debate. But none protested, since the danger was patent.

The next hours passed like a feverish dream. Soon the criers were going through the town. It was the custom for the public slaves to clear the market place at Assembly time by passing through it with a rope dipped in red ruddle so that loiterers might have a mark on them which all would notice. Today the market was already deserted, while the people flocked to the place of their meeting, silent and grim. Leon was awaiting them in the President's seat, his feelings struggling between the weight of disaster and a sense of unreality. This day was as lovely as any other summer day. The outlines of the mountains rose sharply in the crystalline air. The sun was still flashing on the gilded spear of the great Athene on the Acropolis. Yet far away men were dead, had been dead yesterday, dead days before that. Men Leon had grown up with, loved or quarreled with. Rich men, poor men, young men. There had been nothing to mark the special day on which they died. It had been a bright day like this one, when little sparkles of light had caught the tops of the waves all over the bay, when battered merchantmen had come into port from the ends of the earth, bringing news with their cargo.

All the business and tumult of this Assembly was but accompaniment to such thoughts in men's minds. Perhaps as a consequence, these hours slid into each other in memory later. Leon never was certain at what point in that terrible day it came to his attention that the business of being President was not to be ended by the people voting their measures. On this day of all days, barbarian envoys had arrived unannounced from the West. Other persons might go home to be alone with their sorrow. It would be Leon's duty to receive these strangers, lodge them well, and entertain them. After a series of arrangements which he hardly knew he made, he even found himself presiding at a banquet. This was a task which he would have performed in embarrassed silence on any other day, but on this one he was too preoccupied to be self-conscious. Forgetting his diminutive size and his unready tongue, he found himself calmly looking these men over.

There were three of the barbarians, bearded men and sunburned, draped in long, white garments with a purple stripe running down them. By the look of their hands, they farmed their own land. One of them spoke Greek with fair fluency and interpreted for the others.

"We saw men weeping in the streets," this man remarked. "Is somebody dead?"

"An army of ours has been defeated," replied Leon stiffly.

This was interpreted and frowned over. "We do not consider it fitting to mourn defeats in public," the interpreter said. "We prefer to avenge them."

"Indeed!" Leon's tone was barely polite, and the subject dropped. It was now up to Leon to find something else to say, and he made an inquiry into the government of their little city.

"We are a republic now," the interpreter told him. "We used to have kings."

"We, too, had kings many centuries back," agreed Leon more affably, waiting while his remark was repeated in their barbarian tongue. It appeared not to find favor, for the oldest shook his head and frowned.

"We choose two presidents of our republic," the interpreter pursued.

"We choose one." Leon made a little bow. "But the Spartans have two equal kings."

Once again the eldest shook his head over the kings. Leon almost sighed. It was hard work making conversation with one's thoughts elsewhere. His little politenesses seemed to fall very flat with these solemn men. He tried once more. "Every city has its own institutions and laws, none like the other."

The older man nodded at that and said quite intelligibly, "Solon!"

"Why, yes," agreed Leon, surprised. "You have heard of our Solon? He was a very wise man and our greatest lawgiver, but that was a long time ago. We have passed many laws since."

"We have been sent here," the interpreter said, "to study the laws of this Solon."

Leon looked at the three men with a new interest. Theirs was an unusual mission, if only because Solon's laws were so old-fashioned. Nonetheless, they had been the foundation of Athenian justice. If these rustic people had conceived an interest in Solon, why, they had some notion of justice themselves. This was not common among barbarians, who were either savages like the Scythians in the North or slaves of the Persian. Leon wondered what sort of people these Westerners were, yet he felt too weary and despondent to inquire. The sun was setting, and very presently his day of office would be over. He took refuge in a polite gesture and drank to Solon. The three barbarians drank, too, with grave approval.

There were not many minutes left. Leon began a story about the wisdom of Solon. It went very slowly interpreted line by line, and it seemed to lack point. Still, it passed time.

The sun dipped. Leon made his excuses . . . a ritual which he must perform at sunset . . . They must understand. He was impatient for the long day to be over, too tired to consider whether he had done well or ill. He was a small man of no particular importance and had done nothing special in an office which was after all a formality. He wanted to drink the health of their obscure little town before he went, but he could not in his fatigue and confusion remember its name. Suddenly it came to him. He raised his cup as a signal that they, too, should raise theirs and said, "To our two cities." He added, slowly and clearly to make them understand, "To Athens and Rome."

# After-Dinner Stories

## Athens About 450 B.C.

OUR COMPANY had finished dessert and poured an offering to the good spirit. Slave girls had changed the tables and brought rosewater for our hands. This was a refinement of which Aspasia was fond, for by such touches she reminded us that we were dining with a woman. Respectable wives were banned from Athenian dinner parties, but there were pretty young foreign girls like Aspasia whom one could hire. Some of these mixed dinners were little more than disgraceful orgies. Aspasia's parties were simple gatherings of men friends, refined by her presence, spiced by the unexpected, softened in manner. Aspasia was well read. She had studied the poets.

She thought over questions of our day. She had wit as well as grace, accomplishments as well as beauty. Not for Aspasia were the trivial after-dinner games of tossing dregs from cups of wine at a mark, while betting on our skill. She had brought in a flute player to accompany our after-dinner offerings to the gods, to the heroes, and to Zeus. But for the whole evening she would not rely on music either, unless Pericles looked tired.

I glanced at Pericles, who lay next Aspasia, his great domed head supported on his hand. He was smiling at her, which meant merely that Pericles was considerate, even when troubled. He must needs have been uneasy that day because his enemies, despairing of attacking him directly, had laid information against Anaxagoras, his intimate friend. The charge was impiety and might cost Anaxagoras his life, since it was true enough that he in private had informed his friends that by his calculations the sun and the moon were not the chariots of Apollo and his sister Artemis. The sun, Anaxagoras said, was a red-hot mass and the moon a cold, dark one with no light of its own, but reflecting the sun. It would be easy to stir the common people to avenge this insult to the twin immortals. Had not Apollo brought a pestilence on the Greeks before Troy for a far lesser wrong?

Anaxagoras himself looked stubborn tonight. He was a thin, sharp-faced man with a bald head and a full beard touched with gray. On this special occasion, the seriousness of his position had so far impressed him that he was refraining from speech. His lined, lean face, however, conveyed the feeling that he altered no opinion and would not pretend to. He was watching Aspasia. Anaxagoras was of all men least susceptible to the charms of women, but he admired Aspasia's wit and was able to treat her as though she were merely one of his promising pupils.

Aspasia's dark eyes measured her audience almost with an air of challenge. She was not accustomed to let the mood of the company dominate her evening. It was her privilege, moreover, to set the subject of after-dinner conversation or introduce some game of wits. On rare occasions she would delegate this task to someone else, but not tonight. She looked as though she were plotting a surprise, yet was not certain whether she actually dared to spring it on us. Her face was serious, but on her full lips quivered the beginning of a smile, faint and bewitching, as though she was inwardly gay and could not help it.

Our ceremonies came to an end. Our wine was brought to us. The flute player at a nod from Aspasia retired. "My friends," she addressed us all, "we are met to be merry, not solemn; and yet you all sit glum. Then is it not better to talk of what weighs on our minds? The task I shall set you is that each one shall tell us a story or give an opinion about impiety. Now, who will begin?"

She looked at us, lips parted, eyes sparkling, brown face aglow. In the state of public feeling, she might well find herself on trial if news of this discussion leaked out. Aspasia was not respectable; she was foreign; and Peri-

cles loved her. She came from Miletus on the Asian
coast and was thought to urge on Pericles a peace with
Persia and development of trade. Thus social prejudice
and political hatred endangered her position. The super-
stitious fears of the ignorant could destroy her. It was
like Aspasia to risk her life for a whim and to put all of
us into the power of her slaves, who all adored her.
There was a moment of silence. Then Anaxagoras threw
back his head and laughed aloud.

"We are kindred spirits, Aspasia, you and I. Let the
rabble roar. I claim the right to begin, being judged most
impious of this present company. I'll tell you a story."

"Better not," warned Pericles low-voiced. "Leave talk
to others. If the very slightest rumor got abroad . . ."

"My people are discreet," Aspasia protested. She
pouted. "So am I."

"That I take leave to doubt." But Pericles smiled.

Anaxagoras shrugged with real indifference. "If my
life is to hang on discretion, why then I am lost. I have
never had any. But the tale I am going to tell will become common knowledge in the town in any case, since
that fool, Lampon, hardly knows how to hold his tongue,
even should he desire to.

"Well, Pericles has an estate, as you know, on the plain
of Eleusis. I doubt if he goes there twice a year, being
fully occupied in Athens with politics and love and the
conversation of impious fellows like me. On his farm
this year there grew a ram with one horn in the middle

of its forehead. Such strange prodigies, as you know, are thought to have some meaning for men's lives, so that very naturally there was a great stir among the slaves who had reared it. Presently Pericles's steward came here to ask what should be done with the creature.

"Pericles desired to see for himself, and so in fact did I, for very often rumor exaggerates. In this case, however, when the ram arrived, it proved indeed to have one single horn — a heavy, ridged horn proper to a ram and curved as they usually are, but growing exactly in the middle of its forehead. Pericles naturally — and indeed by my advice — showed it to Lampon as the prophet with most reputation here in Athens. Lampon examined it as we had done and, greatly excited, retired to consult his books of prophecy.

"He returned today, full of pomp, and proudly told us with much detail culled from his curious learning that the gods made clear by the single horn that of the two great parties that are struggling to control our state, one should prevail and one vanish. Since, moreover, the ram was Pericles's ram, the gods also intended to show that his should be the victorious party.

"Thus prophesied Lampon, stroking his beard in great complacence because he had discovered why the gods had allowed some ewe to bring forth this strange creature. But I, begging the beast from Pericles for my own experiment, killed it and split open the head. Then I showed Pericles how the brain was malformed and had concentrated in a little space like an egg at the base of that horn. And for that reason, the single horn had grown out as it did."

"This was no impiety to point out fact," Pericles protested. "Indeed, I thought you had the better of Lampon."

Anaxagoras grinned. "Lampon was angry because he looked the fool he is. In time, as we all hope, you will be victorious and guide the state. Then Lampon may boast that he prophesied a truth which I denied. What is my impiety but exposure of men's superstitions?"

Pheidias the sculptor passed a nervous hand over his thinning hair and joined in the argument in the diffident way he had amid men of quicker mind. "Did you really intend to prove Lampon wrong? I cannot see you did so. For if the gods meant that beast to show us the future, they might still have made it with a brain of a peculiar kind which produced one horn."

Anaxagoras shrugged. He regarded Pheidias with a strange, uneasy respect which he paid to no other. Anaxagoras despised illogical beliefs, and in matters of logic the sculptor was very soon out of his depth. Moreover, no one could view the miraculous beauty of Pheidias's images of the gods and doubt his faith. Yet though Anaxagoras took great satisfaction in showing up other men as fools, he usually left Pheidias alone. Like the rest of us, he was awe-stricken by the very majesty of the artist's conceptions. Besides, having greatness of a sort himself, he recognized that quality in others.

Pheidias cleared his throat and smoothed his hair again. He found it difficult to express himself and would puzzle over a problem as though words were strange to him and real ideas could only be properly clothed in bronze or marble. Anaxagoras had little patience at all times, and undoubtedly his peril had sharpened his temper. He had spared Pheidias once. Now he lay waiting with a cold, withdrawn expression which meant that he was pondering one of his bitter retorts, his quiet pieces of rudeness which people found it hard to forgive because they could think of no answer. The poet Sophocles and I, who both loved Pheidias, exchanged dubious glances. An interruption might merely provoke Anaxagoras to more annoyance.

Aspasia leaned forward, smiling. "Anaxagoras has spoken well, but Timon so far has not said a word. Let me tell you, Timon, one needs to put on a bold face with these philosophers, or they will talk all night. We have our experiences as well as they, and we must not withhold them."

She glanced at Anaxagoras, who nodded curtly. "If I have spoken too long, I'm done. Let Timon entertain you."

"If it is to be my turn," I agreed, trying to smooth the matter over, "I'll put you a question about a popular belief, and Anaxagoras may comment if he chooses. You may remember that I too own a farm, in the district of Acharnae. Unlike Pericles, I am my own manager; and I am always out there for the plowing and the vine or

olive harvests, and often in between. My nearest neighbor was a very rustic little elderly fellow called Polemon,
who wasn't above working his tiny fields with one slave
or even hiring himself out to help with our harvest when
his own was gathered in. In fact, one would have hardly
known Polemon from a slave, were it not that sometimes
he would pluck me by the cloak and breathe his garlic in
my face while we chatted of the weather, his wife's bad
leg, his lucky amulet, or the cock he sacrificed to the god
of health, and how such meat on feast days made a
change, though it was seldom he had it. Thus he proved
his free-born status by confiding his affairs to me after the
fashion of simple folk who understand conversation as
talking about themselves. Having done so in full sight
of my people, he felt his dignity permitted him to work
with the rest.

"In this casual way, without thinking much of it,
I learned a good deal about Polemon over the years. He
was a kindly fellow, got on with his wife, lived almost as
an equal with his slave, and was as honest as any farmer
who has a hard time making ends meet. That is to say,
he did not steal; but if our boundary line could be moved
a foot or two in my direction, he may have done it. He
was full of simple piety and little recipes for extracting
favor from the gods or avoiding bad luck. If a cat crossed
Polemon's path, he had to stop and toss three stones. If
he heard an owl hoot, he must call on Athene at once.
Every snake of the sacred sort on his land must have its
shrine. Poor as he was, there was always a skin of wine

or a flask of oil kept for the diviner, who must explain his dreams and reassure him that he was on good terms with the gods and going to prosper. In short, to sum Polemon up, he was inoffensive, cheerful, hard-working, anxious to please. Of positive virtues he may not have had a great share, since he was too poor to contribute much time or thought to the state; but if there was harm in him, I never found any.

"Now three years ago at the time of the autumn plowing, as this Polemon worked in his fields, he was killed by lightning. The thunderbolts of Zeus are a terrible weapon and very rarely used on a human being. One would have imagined that their victim must be a parricide, a notorious breaker of a very solemn oath, or an offender against the gods of some other serious sort. Must we class Polemon with wicked men like these, or did the god miss his mark? Or shall we say with Anaxagoras that the thunder is an explosion caused by the heat in the upper air, and that the lightning is not directed by the god, but hits at random?"

"In fact, it is hardly a question of whether Polemon was an impious man," Pericles smiled, "but of whether we are so ourselves. For if the thunderbolt was of Zeus, then the god in a rage or a drunken fit must have slain a harmless man for sport or missed his mark. Dare we suggest such a thing of Zeus? If, however, we conclude that the lightning has nothing to do with the god, our state is still worse."

I nodded, appreciating the way that the politician in

him had avoided a dangerous opinion and had at the
same time spared Anaxagoras from giving any. "We
cease to be truly pious the moment we bring our minds
to bear on this problem."

"Th-the gods are not to be understood in this way,"
protested Pheidias. He made a gesture with both hands
as though he were literally shaping his thought in the air.
"They are . . . they are felt."

"Just so," Pericles agreed. "Yet these questions must be
asked."

"Sophocles asks them," Aspasia put in. "His plays are
full of them. Are they not, Sophocles?"

The poet nodded his handsome head. "And yet the
end of it is that I agree with Pheidias. The gods are not
rational, nor are their ways understandable to reason. If
it were not too long, I would tell you a story I once heard
in Samos which illustrates some questions about what
impiety is . . . but I should tire you."

"No story from Sophocles tires," Aspasia assured him.
"And if it really is long, I daresay Pericles and possibly
Pheidias, too, will surrender their turns."

"I'll do it gladly," Pheidias agreed. "We all know who
is the teller of magical stories, just as we also know who is
the sharpest in argument — and who is the dullest." He
smiled gently at Anaxagoras, who nodded to him as if to
say, "In spite of all, we two have something in common."

"I could listen to Sophocles all night," said Pericles.

"You flatter me." But Sophocles spoke abstractedly,
his hand fingering his beard as he plainly considered

what the details of his story were and how it began.

"In the days when Polycrates was ruling in Samos, there lived a man on that island whose name was Ariston. Now the time of Polycrates was a great one for Samos, so much so that men still look back to that glorious age. Ariston, therefore, was lucky in the place of his birth and lucky also in that he was born to great wealth. When he grew to manhood, he was lucky again, since his father married him to a woman of great beauty whom he loved dearly. Therewith, his luck ran out, for he had no sons.

"He waited for five years with growing impatience. Then he took his wife to the temple at Ephesus and thence to other famous shrines where women go to pray for children. No offerings availed; and after five more years had gone by, the woman was still barren. Ariston's friends had long ago advised him to put her away and take another wife, yet so far he had resisted because he loved her. At last after ten years he spoke of divorce.

"The woman wept very bitterly, for she too loved her husband; but she saw that his mind was made up. She begged him, however, to go at least to Delphi and ask the priestess of Apollo if nothing could be done. Then Ariston, parting from her with great sorrow, did her bidding and sailed away to Delphi, bearing with him a glorious golden cup to offer to the god.

"He waited some weeks at Delphi while he purified himself, sacrificed oxen, and did all possible to win Apollo's favor. But when the seventh day of the month

came round and the holy priestess took her seat on the
sacred tripod to give the answers of the god, she told him
thus:

He who asks what he does not have should consider
Whether he is better off with what he has now.

"This saying angered Ariston, for he did not understand it. Did the god intend to tell him that a second
wife would be worse than the first? Or did Apollo mean
that he would be better off without a son? In any case,
he had still no certainty what he should do or whether he
would have a child. Finally Ariston went to the priests
and begged them to let him ask his question again. This
they consented to do; and a month later when the holy
day arrived, he once more attended. This time the priestess was in a frenzied state, so that she shrieked and
rocked herself on the tripod as the power of the god took
hold. The words she uttered, if they were words at all,
meant nothing to Ariston. But the priests, who were
skilled at such things, interpreted her sayings as:

Rash man to demand of Apollo a second time an answer.
Go home, and you shall learn the power of the god.

"Sadly then Ariston sailed home, not having received
any answer to the question with which he came and being troubled in his mind about the threat of the power of
the god. But when he came to his house, his heart was
filled with rejoicing, for his wife had conceived at last
and was now in her fourth month. She would not show
herself to him, however, but sent word she had dreamed

that if she did so before the child was born, it would die. In his gladness, Ariston made little of that. He busied himself in sending great gifts to Apollo, counting the days till his son should be born and never doubting that the favor of the god would bring him a boy.

"The time of waiting went by, and the woman was delivered of a fine and healthy son who was named Apollodoros because Ariston said the child was a gift of Apollo.

"Now at last Ariston was happy, and he was even more triumphant when within a very few months his wife conceived again. He laughed, but she wept; and when her second son was laid beside her, she implored that this child, too, should have the honor of being called given by a god. Ariston was in a mood to grant her whatever she pleased. He called the baby Theodotos and made a feast for him, less than he had done for his first-born, yet still a great one.

"Thus Ariston attained his desire; and with two fine sons less than a year apart, he thought himself happy. But Apollodoros and his brother Theodotos were at enmity before they could walk or talk. For a few years theirs seemed babyish jealousy which would wear out, but presently their naughtiness increased as they grew and divided the whole household. Ariston favored his eldest-born, while the mother spoiled the younger. Thus husband and wife, who had loved each other so long, began to quarrel. Next, as is always the way, the slaves took sides. The house of Ariston, which had been a happy one, was filled with jealousy, bitterness, and intrigue. The woman, who had been such a great beauty, lost her looks and grew thin and shrewish. As for Ariston, since he was unhappy at home, he went adventuring in the galleys of Polycrates, which preyed on merchantmen of Syria and Phoenicia and Asia Minor.

"Time went by in this way till the boys became young men, still hating each other. The woman died; and in the very same month, Ariston was killed in a sea fight, leaving possessions which had been greatly increased by his years of piracy. There was in fact more than enough to divide, yet Apollodoros conspired with the head steward to cheat his brother. Theodotos for his part took a solemn oath that his mother on her deathbed had confessed that Apollodoros was not her child, but that she had taken the baby of one of her slaves to deceive her husband because he had threatened divorce. Whether this was so or not could not be established, since all the parties were dead. Nor was it certain that the mother was conscious at the last or had spoken to her son. There was a great deal of talk in Samos, some taking one side, some the other. In the end, Theodotos announced that he would appeal to Apollo at Delphi.

"This brought opinion round to the side of Theodotos, since it was reckoned that he would not have dared to appeal to the god unless he spoke truth. Theodotos, however, as was later discovered, had actually lied. His mother had died without confirming or denying the suspicion which he had long held against Apollodoros. Thus when he ventured to go to Delphi for the truth, he was afraid of the god's answer, not that he suspected Apollodoros to be his brother, but that he had already taken a false oath.

"Theodotos, therefore, arrived at Delphi in good time, as his father had done. But instead of haunting the temple with sacrifices and prayers, he conferred secretly with one of the younger priests and offered him a fortune if he would allow him to meet with the holy priestess. Then, some say by a further bribe, while others say by trading on his youth and good looks, he won over the priestess to declare Apollodoros no true son of Ariston.

"In this way Theodotos drove his brother out; and Apollodoros in fear and rage left the country, lest he be adjudged to be the born slave of his brother. It was his intention to enter the service of the Great King; but while he was traveling between Ephesus and Sardis, he fell among robbers, who killed him for the money he had on him.

"Theodotos now possessed his father's wealth with none to say that he had not full right to it. But he had not much enjoyment therefrom, since time and again he was visited with agonizing boils which drove him almost out of his mind with pain. Even Democedes, the famous doctor of Croton, whom Polycrates had attracted to his court, could not relieve him. In despair at last, Theodotos went to Epidaurus, where the temple of the god of healing is. There he did not dare give his name to the priests; but he mingled with the poor and the sick who slept in the precinct nightly, praying for visions.

Many nights Theodotos slept there; but though other
people were comforted and healed by their dreams, he
himself was neglected.

"At last he could bear no more, but confessed to the
priests his name and the place from whence he came and
the name of his father. Then the god spoke to him in the
night and bade him be gone, for none could heal him
save Apollo, who had laid this sickness on him.

"Theodotos went away in fear and pain. Returning to
Samos, he took half the wealth he had from his father
and with it made vessels of gold for the temple of the god.
Thus bearing a gift such as few private men had ever
offered, he went to Delphi to ask mercy of Apollo.

"There was a new priestess this year, for Apollo had
visited the old one with a frenzy in which she died.
When this woman saw Theodotos, she began to scream
and foam at the mouth and spit at him, crying:

Cursed be he who swore a false oath to another man's
    ruin.
Cursed be he who bribed the servants of Apollo.

Then she threw herself from the tripod and lay like one
dead.

"The priests dragged Theodotos away from the holy
place, but they dared not thrust him outside the temple
precinct while he called on the name of Apollo. Nor
would Theodotos leave, but he vowed he would die where
he was and pollute the temple. For a month he lay there,

tended by the priests, who feared the defilement which must be caused by his death, but yet were unwilling to turn away a suppliant, however guilty. The end of it was that another man was induced to ask the priestess how Theodotos might be healed and what should be done.

"This time Apollo answered that Theodotos might find healing at the touch of any man who had sinned more terribly against the gods than he.

"Theodotos now had himself carried out of the temple, for his disease was worse in the house of Apollo. Thereafter, he sailed back to Samos and sold all he still had, vowing half of it to Apollo when he should be healed, and half to the man who should cure him. Then he sent messengers throughout Greece, inviting any man to come and heal him. Meanwhile, he himself made inquiries to discover what sort of crime might seem more offensive to the gods than his own.

"Some said one thing, and some said another. It was easier, however, to think of crimes than to discover men who had done them. Either such men were dead or outlawed, or they were unwilling to expose their guilt at all. Even in cases where notorious wrongs had been committed, the guilty hesitated to lay their hands on Theodotos, lest by so doing they admit their wickedness had no excuse. At all events, in spite of the money Theodotos offered, and in spite of the fact that men of that age were no less evil than now, few came forward to try their powers of healing, and all failed. At last Theodotos was forced to set out on his travels again and, ill as he was, to drag himself through the length and breadth of Greece.

"Some years he spent in this way, traveling either on foot or by ship, or with bearers, according as his sickness waxed or waned. In every city he came to, he would seek out people who were suspected of wrongdoing. But wherever a man had committed a great crime, he dared not admit it, and more laid hands on Theodotos to prove their innocence than to earn a reward at the price of confessing their guilt. Despairing, therefore, Theodotos still dragged himself from town to town, unable to give up the search, or to die, or to be cured.

"He was being carried through the hills of Thessaly, not far from Delphi itself, when he fell among robbers. His bearers, who were nothing but hired men, put him down and ran away. The outlaws fell on him and began to jostle him about, snatching at his cloak and his cushions, his bag of provisions, and everything that lay around him. And suddenly, as they all had their hands on him at once, he felt himself healed.

"Theodotos sprang up with a great cry, so frightening the robbers that they dropped what they had taken up and ran away. The more Theodotos besought them to stop, the more they panicked. Theodotos, however, in the first flush of his restored strength came up with the oldest, who was the slowest of foot, and grappled with him. Then partly by persuasion and partly by threats, he induced him to summon the rest. Presently, when they approached him somewhat timorously, he told them

that to one or other of them he owed a great sum
of money.

"They did not believe him.

" 'He is a spy come to hunt us down,' cried one.

" 'He is delaying us here while his friends surround
us.'

" 'Kill him!' demanded the third.

" 'Take me with you wherever you wish,' cried Theodotos. 'And when you think yourselves safe, let me question you. For to one of you I owe half what I own, and I
must pay it.'

"They took him at last to a little cave in the hills where
they lived, trapping small game, gathering berries, and
robbing passers-by whenever they dared. Here they sat
in their miserable rags and stared at Theodotos, each
keeping his knotted club by his side, as though uncertain
whether it would not be better to kill him and divide
what he had on him.

" 'Tell me now,' said Theodotos to them, 'since all of
you are outlaws and have nothing to lose by confessing
your crimes, what is it you have done? For to him whom
the gods have cursed, I owe my money.'

"Then said the first, 'I killed my father.'

"Said the second, 'I robbed my master.'

"The third said, 'I dragged my enemy from the sacred
precinct and killed him.'

"The fourth said, 'I betrayed my native city.'

"Theodotos thought for a moment, wondering whether
under their uncut hair and tangles of beard he could pos-

sibly trace out the features of him whom the gods had cursed. Then he said to the first, 'Tell me how you killed your father.'

" 'A madness seized on him,' said the man, 'so that he caught up an axe and ran at me, crying that he would slay me. Then I struck at the axe with a stick and, missing, dashed his brains out.'

"Theodotos stared into his eyes, which were terribly reddened and inflamed from the smoke in the cave. But after a minute he turned away from him and said to the second, 'Tell me how you robbed your master.'

" 'I was a priest in a great temple,' said he, 'and I stole pieces of the robe of the image, which was of beaten gold.'

"Theodotos nodded and said to the third one, 'Who was your enemy, and why did you kill him?'

"The man said, 'I had a friend whom I loved, and we were far closer than brothers. This man murdered him, and therefore I killed him.'

"Then Theodotos said to the fourth, 'Why did you betray your native city?'

" 'Our enemies captured me and put me to the torture to make me betray a secret path up the ramparts.'

"Theodotos thought once again, and he looked from one to the other, finding little to choose between their miseries. These men went barefoot, their rags scarcely hung together, and their limbs were skin and bone. Yet the god had laid on him the task of discovering which one was truly most wretched. So for the third time he questioned them and said to the first one, 'If the death of

your father was by accident, could you not have purged
yourself of blood-guilt, dreadful though your deed was?'

" 'This was not granted me,' said the man, 'because the
potion which sent my father mad was of my providing.
An old witch gave it me to persuade him that I should
marry a woman whom I loved.'

"Then Theodotos turned to the second one and asked
him, 'How dared you despoil the very image of the god?'

" 'Because our shrine was a place of oracles,' said the
man, 'and once I sold a false answer to one of the
pilgrims. Then since nothing happened to me, I grew
bolder, thinking that the god and his oracle alike were
only a sham.'

"Theodotos peered at him sharply, but so pinched were
his features by want, so filthy was he that no resemblance
to the priest at Delphi remained, if indeed this was the
man.

" 'If your enemy was a murderer,' said he to the third
man, 'could you not have left him to the city, or to the
god?'

" 'He was condemned to die,' the robber said, 'and
men were leading him outside the city to the place of execution. But he broke from the hands of those who held
him and ran to the temple of Hera. He had no time to
open the gates of the precinct because we were hard on
his heels, but he took hold of the handles of the doors and
clung to them, crying out on the name of the goddess.
Then the executioners tried to drag him away, but could
not do so and were perhaps afraid to try very hard. So I

took out my sword and hacked his hands off at the wrists; and leaving these to clutch the temple door, I dragged my enemy to execution.'

"Then Theodotos said to the last man, 'What did your enemies do to your native city?'

" 'They killed the men,' said he with tears in his eyes. 'They enslaved the women and plundered the temples. Then they sent colonists of their own to live in it.'

"Theodotos looked at them all again in turn from the first to the last. Then quietly he turned to the man whom the gods had cursed and said, 'I will pay you the money.' "

Sophocles lay back on his cushions, and there was a silence for a moment because the ending had taken us by surprise.

"Oh, Sophocles," protested Aspasia, laughing, "you never heard that story in Samos, no matter what you pretend to spare our praises. And now you have left us to guess who was accursed."

"If you will tell me who he was," retorted Sophocles with twinkling eyes, "I could finish the story. But my informant in Samos did not know."

"Must it not be the first man?" I asked. "It is true that he did not kill his father by intent, but he was guilty of sending him mad. Besides, the gods judge by the deed, not the motive as men do. Surely parricide is in their eyes the most shocking of crimes."

"I hardly think so," remarked Anaxagoras sourly. "Zeus killed his own father Cronos, as our legends say. No, the gods care little about crimes if popular tales have any truth in them. In fact, if the gods are really such as people think them, then the thieving priest must be the guilty one. The gods are more jealous of anything which concerns themselves than they are of crimes against mere mortals."

"That may be so," Pheidias admitted. "Yet I think the third man committed a crime against both gods and men. To cut off a suppliant's hands!"

Aspasia nodded her head. "It is an offense against the very nature of the gods. Pheidias is right. The gods show pity to every suppliant and must therefore shudder at cruelty. Is it not so, Pericles?"

"You are all wrong." Pericles lifted himself on his elbow. "It is the fourth man, though he was not a criminal and gave way under torture. For he betrayed to death his father and brothers, and sold his mother into slavery. He robbed the images of the gods. He slew the suppliants on the steps of their own altars. And the city, which we may suppose a fair one, or at all events fair to him, was destroyed and resettled. It would have been better for that man if he had killed himself or if he had never been born. What are we but citizens? What are our lives apart from the city for which we work, through which we win glory, and for which we die?"

Aspasia lifted the garland she wore on her head and put it gently on the head of Pericles. As for Sophocles, he said, "I did not know the answer, but our Pericles can persuade me of anything. It was the fourth man."

# The Adventure of the Merchant's Son

## Athens and Byzantium 431 B.C.

My FATHER Philemon was a corn merchant in a small way, having risen in this business from a state of destitution. I have often wondered what may have been in our ancestry which caused the gods to visit us with ill-luck in each generation. For my grandfather Philo, being struck on the head by a tile which blew off his roof in a great storm, died some weeks too early to be killed in the sea battle off Salamis. Thus Philemon, unlike most orphans of that time, was not made a ward of the state. Meanwhile, the Persian pulled down the roof which had killed Philo, cut his olive trees, and plundered his possessions. After the battle, when Athens was resettled, Philemon's mother was forced to desperate straits to support herself. To be frank, she had for many years a stall in the public

market where she sold ribbons. Philemon put a stop to
this when he was old enough, but the disgrace of it clung
about him to his dying day and gave him a reluctance to
show himself in the city of Athens. He lived in the
Piraeus, where I remember my grandmother well, a little, stout old lady, hoarse-voiced and quick of temper.
She ruled us all by the virulence of her tongue, often forcing my mother to clap shocked hands to her ears and run
away.

Philemon, being brought up in this way amid the low-
est class of porter, cloak snatcher, beggar, or hawker, soon
took service in the fleet to better himself. After serving
as an oarsman several years, he had the good fortune to
attract his captain's notice and get promotion, eventually
becoming a pilot and master. Thence he passed to spec-
ulation in goods returning to Athens, which he sometimes had opportunity to pick up cheap. Investing his
profits in a part share in a merchant ship, he prospered
and after a while bought the ship and the oarsmen. He
never, as far as I know, owned his cargo completely, but
would borrow money to finance every trip, which he re-
paid from the return cargo. He had gradually come to
concentrate on the corn trade with the Bosporos and the
Black Sea. This trade was large and vital to the state. The
profits were modest, but certain. Money could be borrowed at much more reasonable rates than for big specu-
lations. Besides, the corn trade was a profession in itself.
Philemon had his contacts at Byzantium on the Bosporos
and at all the ports of the Black Sea as far east as Sinope.

Likewise in the Piraeus he had his banker and his backers, his favorite grain dealers, his suppliers of armor or wine or olive oil and similar exports, depending on the season, the chances of war, and other local issues up north which it was his profession to discover. Philemon's trade was small, but his reputation was better by far than that of the resident aliens who formed large companies for trading from the Piraeus.

Such was the business of Philemon. I myself knew little of it, for it was my father's ambition to restore us to the prosperous farming class of my grandfather Philo. My mother was of this class, and I had early been sent to my uncle's in Athens, where I might, my father said, go to school with decent people instead of all the riffraff of the Piraeus. My uncle was comparatively well-to-do, and I have since concluded that my father strained his resources to have me brought up on equality with my cousins.

In this way for many years I saw little of my parents. My father was often away and very seldom when he came into port went up to Athens. As for my mother, she was quite occupied with her woman's work and with bringing up my sister. From my own point of view, the Piraeus was within an easy walk; but I had little leisure and was not encouraged by my elders to go thither. When my schooldays were over, I must of course do my military training. I was outfitted for the cavalry because my cousins were so, although as I later heard, Philemon's losses at this time made the expense a burden.

The beginning of Philemon's misfortunes was caused by a shipwreck which he brought on himself by venturing too early on the seas before the winter's storms were over. A recent quarrel between Byzantium and the king of Thrace had put a premium on arms and armor. One of Philemon's friends who owned a shield factory in the Piraeus had recently died; and, owing to various squabbles between his heirs, the shields were going cheap. Tempted thus by a cargo which would command a good price, particularly at the beginning of the season, Philemon took a risk and lost both ship and cargo. It was a disaster he could ill afford. To be sure, the money he had borrowed on the shields was not repayable unless his ship came safe to port. However, he had ventured money of his own as well, while the ship was almost a new one which he had built at his own cost. He was not able to afford another ship, but he rented out his oarsmen and himself took passage with another merchant as supercargo and part owner of a consignment of goods. Thus for a few seasons he traded on a reduced scale, always hoping that some lucky coup would restore his fortunes.

My own involvement with Philemon's affairs began with a chance conversation as we were camping out near the Boeotian border close to the end of my military training. We had been riding all day and were sweaty and tired, but the servant whom my tent mates and I owned in common was grooming our horses. Our tent was already pitched, and supper was ready. We ate and relaxed, idly picturing ourselves as free to do whatever we pleased when our training was over.

"I shall marry," Antiphon declared. "My father wishes it, and his cousin has a daughter of suitable age. She's said to be pretty."

"With a suitable dowry, I hope," remarked Agoratos.

"Of course."

Agoratos shrugged. "Well, I shan't marry early. I don't want to settle down yet. There's too much going on."

"Parties and talk?"

"Certainly talk." Agoratos grinned. "I'm going to take lessons in public speaking. That's a necessity for success in politics nowadays. Then there'll be some chorus to produce, a ship to outfit, and a campaign to serve on. Life's too interesting to tie oneself down with some girl hardly out of her childhood."

"I'm going to write plays," Aristophanes volunteered. He was only seventeen and just beginning his service, but we had adopted him because he was a cousin of Agoratos.

"What makes you think you're the new Euripides, eh?" jeered Agoratos.

"Comic plays, not tragic ones, my friend. When you're the new Pericles, I'll skin you alive onstage before the whole Athenian people."

"I wouldn't be surprised if he did, too," agreed Antiphon, "with that sharp tongue."

"But what about Philo?" Agoratos turned around on me. "You're very silent."

I leaned back on the grass and looked at the sky, in which the first star had just come out. "I wish I knew. I'm worried."

"If it's the money I lent you," Agoratos said, "forget it. I'm tiding you over while your father's away. I'm not in a hurry."

I considered. "No, it isn't the money, though it's awkward not getting any. It's just . . . well, I don't know anything about my father's business. I don't even know exactly where he is at this time. He's been away all summer."

"Has he?" protested Agoratos, surprised. "I thought you said . . ."

"Perhaps he did come into port and go again without letting me know. His ways never bothered me before, but now . . . I can't live with my uncle after I'm grown. Besides, he's gone with the embassy to Corcyra."

"Why don't you ask for leave?" Aristophanes suggested. "Go home for a few days. At least you can discover when your father will be due and why no one answered your message. If you had the reputation of being a terrible, wild fellow, Philo, they'd not dare treat you so. You're too good-natured."

I shrugged off this remark, but I thought it was true. I was getting annoyed by slow, imperceptible stages. The nuisance of hot and dusty travel from the frontier and finding stabling for my horse increased this to anger. Uncertain of my welcome, puzzled, truculent, I shouldered my way through the crowds of the Piraeus, came at last to my father's door, and found it ajar.

I could hardly believe my eyes. We had a porter, not for display, but to protect the women in my father's absences. His lodge was empty. There had been across the passage an office where my father transacted business because his acquaintances were sometimes rough and he did not wish to bring them through the open court to the men's apartment. I looked inside, and it was bare of furniture. Surely my father would not have moved his house without bothering to tell me!

Three strides brought me into the court. There was nothing in it but rubbish and the small central altar. No bird cage, no toys of my sister's, no bedding spread to air, no basket for my mother's spinning, no signs of work or even habitation. I glanced in the alcove . . . and there my grandmother stood, looking silently at me.

She had been dead ten years, but for a moment with my eyes dazzled by the sun, I thought she was a vision. Then as I blinked and gulped, the figure spoke.

"So you've come," she said sourly. "At last. I suppose you want more money."

The voice brought me to my senses. "Aglaia! My sister! I didn't recognize you at first. How you've grown!" I peered at her crossly, by no means pleased at what I saw. Her dumpy figure and square, heavy-set jaw were both my grandmother to the life, as was her bitter tongue. "Why, we'll have to be thinking of a dowry for you, Aglaia," I said with the false gaiety appropriate for greeting a little sister after two years and finding her grown up — though less attractive than I liked to say. Aglaia did not smile.

"There isn't any money," she said. "And there never will be now. As for you, you've spent your last copper."

"What's going on here?" I demanded roughly, all my anxieties, my resentments, my hot journey sharpening my tone. "Mind your manners, Aglaia. Is this the way for a modest girl to speak to her elder brother? I'm ashamed of you. Where's my mother? And where's my father?"

She thrust out that determined chin the way Grandmother did. "Mother's asleep and not to be wakened. Father . . ." I saw her lips tremble a little. "Father's dead."

"He's WHAT?" I could hardly believe my own ears. "Why wasn't I told?"

She shrugged — a mulish gesture. "Nothing to tell. We are sure Philemon's dead. But they say — they say he ran away with a lot of money and disappeared. He'd never do that."

I did not know Philemon well, but I knew his reputation in my uncle's eyes was that of an honest man. I had never questioned this and did not now. My indignation was immediate and prompt. "Who tells these lies about him?"

She considered a moment. "Well, there's Glaucon, from whose ship he vanished. And Sosias. It's Sosias's money."

Sosias was a slave name. It was not Philemon's habit to

borrow from the aliens and freedmen who did a great
part of the Piraeus's trade. He said those people all knew
each other too well and skinned you alive. But when I
commented on this, Aglaia told me that beggars could
not be choosers. "With an idle, spendthrift son never
earning a penny, what was Philemon to do? Oh, we've
gone hungry, but you must have enough for all your
pleasures."

"Why didn't he tell me?"

"If you'd been home just once in the last two years,
you'd have seen for yourself."

It was true enough, but how should I have come, never
knowing when my father was at home, save in the win-
ters when I was on garrison duty and travel at its worst?
Besides, he never came to see me, did not welcome me
in the Piraeus, which he said was not my proper sphere.
What Aglaia thought luxury were the commonplaces of
living in my uncle's house, while my extravagances had
been modest beside those of young men I knew. There
was excuse for me, but I would not say so to Aglaia. The
disappearance of Philemon and the straits to which my
mother and sister seemed reduced were so appalling that
I had no time to spare for clearing up misunderstandings.

"What happened to him?" I said. "Leave my part in
our misfortunes and come to Philemon. When and
where did he vanish?"

"He sailed for Byzantium," she said, "with this man
Glaucon. He was carrying a thousand jars of perfumed
oil—those very small ones. There are fashions in per-

fume, and one of the dealers up there wished to corner a market. Philemon had trouble in finding so much, but he expected a good profit because the corn dealers up in Byzantium were overstocked from last year, while the new harvest in all the Black Sea lands was reported to be bountiful. Wishing, therefore, to take up most of Glaucon's ship, Philemon added for the outward voyage skins of Chian wine which he merely hoped to dispose of at cost because last season . . ."

"Why, you talk like a clerk," I said, wondering. "Who taught you to understand men's business?"

She scowled. "Philemon liked to explain and I to listen. What harm was there? He had no son to confide in."

"His fault, not mine," I told her sharply, wondering what my mother had been about to permit such folly. It would be a problem to marry any girl off after such an upbringing.

"Well, Aglaia?"

"He needed a large loan, but none of the bankers were willing to trust a man whom misfortune had dogged for these last years. It is their business to estimate a merchant's luck. But the freedman Sosias in the end advanced it."

"And then?"

"Then Philemon sailed to Byzantium with Glaucon, sold his cargo, and was paid it seems in silver, not by banker's draft. Then he vanished."

"Knocked on the head and thrown in the harbor?"

"So I suppose, but they say . . . they say there was a woman with whom he always lodged, and that she disappeared with him. I don't believe it."

"Who told this story? Glaucon?" I asked indignantly. "I'll make him eat it."

She looked at me, brows slightly raised. "He'd break you in two. Nor does it matter greatly what Glaucon says. It will not bring our father back again. The *Dolphin* returned to harbor safe, and therefore the money which Sosias loaned Philemon is still owing. It was Sosias who came and plundered us of slaves and furniture and what little silver Philemon had left in the house for our expenses."

"Then I'll see Sosias first. Meanwhile, you and my mother . . ."

She stuck her chin out again. "I'll manage. I had hidden a little."

"You'll do as you're told," I said roughly. "You're a woman. Mind your business." It was obvious that Aglaia and my mother must go to my uncle's. The steward would take them in if I ordered him to do so. As for the hoard which Aglaia had saved from our creditors, I intended to use it myself for several things.

The first of these was a talk with Sosias, whom I found without any trouble sitting at a banker's table in the portico which faces onto the docks at the Piraeus. He was a swarthy, hook-nosed fellow whose slave origin had given him a fawning manner. He was all smoothness and flattery as long as he thought I was a wealthy young

man with money to change, but when he discovered who
I was, he altered his tune.

"Two talents of silver, d'you hear! Two talents of silver!" He shook his finger under my nose. "I want my
money, and I'm a bad man to cross. Don't walk the
Piraeus alone on a dark night. I give you fair warning."

"You might find your own nose slit," I said indignantly. No one had ever threatened me with bullies before; and that such a person, not even a Greek, should
abuse me so was very galling.

He gave a little nod, and two enormous brawny slaves
lounged forward round his table.

"We've a short way with thieves," he said. "We throw
'em in the harbor."

It was time for me to back down. I was out of my
depth and also very young. "I'll pay you the money
when I find out where it's gone. I haven't got it."

"You can raise it from your uncle if you want to." He
looked me up and down from my sandals of fine leather
to my cavalry cloak, almost new, and my fashionable
haircut. "And you'd better."

"I'll see what I can do when he comes home." I backed
away, uneasy, ashamed of myself, and seething inwardly.
If Sosias knew the names of my father's customers in
Byzantium, or if he had any suspicion of what might
have happened there, I should not hear it from him. He
clearly thought his silver lost and was only concerned
with wringing as much of it as he could out of me. I
should not have gone to him in my good clothes, or per-

haps not at all. It would have been wiser to send some older man who talked his language.

I wandered up and down the bankers' tables, trying to chance on someone who had dealt with Philemon and knew him well. Many did so, no doubt; but my confidence was shaken. I felt out of place and conspicuous. My manner was awkward, and all soon knew who I was. No doubt that the scandal of Philemon's disappearance had gone up and down the porticoes and been the talk of the port. That some were skeptical of it I could see, and yet the general opinion undoubtedly was that Philemon's affairs were desperate enough for him to consider setting up in another name a long way off. What surprised me was that no friend of his came forward; but Philemon had been a dour, close man. He had considered himself somewhat superior to his fellows and had held aloof. He had married above him and begotten a fine young gentleman for a son with whom no mariner or businessman felt confidential.

The result was, after a fruitless day, I was forced to abate my pride and ask Aglaia who were my father's friends and what his connections. Aglaia knew the answers, even down to the dealers in Byzantium with whom Philemon mainly traded. She did not know, however, which of the sea captains were in town and which not. She suggested that my father's barber for a suitable bribe would inform me. It took days to get this barber alone. I tried to catch him very late or very early, only to find a lounger standing by all ears. In my inexperience, I had not the wits to show my money early; and the barber, who knew very well who I was, may have thought that I had none. At all events, it was done at last. The barber's opinion, which interested me very much, was that Glaucon, the master of the *Dolphin*, had the silver and had paid some bully to kill Philemon for it.

"You'll not bring it home to him," the barber said. "Glaucon's careful. He'll lay up the money until he has a voyage which could account for sudden wealth. But he might be careful in other ways, too. They expect him to be back in port before long. It might be safer to remove yourself to Athens."

I was getting used to the Piraeus by now, and this second threat did not disturb me as much as Sosias had done. I considered. "I'm taking my mother and sister to Athens," I said. "A cart's coming tomorrow for the little they have left. Could you put it about that I've gone with them? Maybe my uncle when he returns will pay our debt, and maybe he won't. In the meanwhile, I don't quite like my haircut. Can you make it less elaborate?"

He winked. "I can give you a brown stain, too. Lucky your complexion's so clear. I might pluck your eyebrows. Better not be seen on the waterfront where you're already known. I'll give you a birthmark."

"How soon will the brown wash off on a sea voyage?"

He thought a little over that and told me I could renew it at Lemnos and Imbros when I went ashore. I tipped him heavily, and he even knew a person who would warn me when this Glaucon came to town and would introduce me as a young man seeking passage to his uncle, who was a trader in Byzantium. He provided me with the name of a Byzantine merchant who might prove a suitable uncle. This last was a favor beyond price. I tried to thank him.

"I liked Philemon," he said unexpectedly. "You've a look of him, too."

I was rather taken aback. I had come to the conclusion that Philemon had no friends. This barber, always in the center of idle chat, had not seemed likely to appeal much to Philemon as I knew him.

The haircut and the stain transformed my appearance, at least to a casual glance. They had, however, an effect we had not foreseen. They intensified my likeness to my father. "Luckily," the barber said, "Philemon was bearded. But it's a risk all the same. Glaucon's no fool."

"I'm going," I insisted. "I have a new name and a convincing story. I'm sailing with the *Dolphin* to Byzantium, and I'll see what I find out there. My father would never lie quiet in his grave, wheresoever it be, if I did less."

He clapped me on the shoulder. "You're a chip off the old block after all. I never would have thought it."

I would not have thought it myself, but strange necessities were bringing out sides to my nature which surprised me. I had not imagined, for instance, how I should thrill to the creaking of the stays as the *Dolphin*'s big sail filled, or how contentedly I should watch the oar blades bite with the unhurried motion that the slaves could keep up hour after hour. I sat on the poop, which was decked, and I saw the golden helmet of Athene flash goodbye to us from the Acropolis. The wind, unrestricted by hill or dale or building, was sweeping the *Dolphin* out to sea like a scattered leaf.

It was the wind, not the sun or the changing water, which made me aware that my life must be spent on the sea. What folly of my father's to have me brought up a gentleman instead of taking me with him and teaching me his trade! Ah well, it was only too likely that I should end up where Philemon was now. I did not like the look of Glaucon or the gaze he bent on me.

The captain of the *Dolphin* was a huge man, so large that his size was an inconvenience on shipboard. He had the habit of hunching himself together as though to apologize for taking so much room. He moved about slowly, like a man who has learned caution by bruising himself. These tricks made him appear quite stupid, yet he noticed my likeness to my father at once. As soon as the bustle of departure was over and our course set fair for Cape Sunium, he sat down beside me and began to inquire into my affairs. I had my story pat, how my father was a resident alien who owned a small factory in Athens. As I was the youngest of three sons, he had determined to send me to Byzantium as apprentice to my uncle, who had recently been bereft of his own heir. This plausible tale accounted for my modest means, my accent, somewhat purer than the dialects of the Piraeus, and even the late age at which I was sent off to become an apprentice. Glaucon listened as I rattled it off, and he said, "Have you no relatives that are Athenian born? I must tell you that you have a great look of an old friend of mine, a man named Philemon."

I felt my color come up. To cover my confusion, I laughed and said directly, "Philemon? Was that not the sea captain you lost on your last voyage? Was there not some mystery about his disappearance? People whispered to me that you were a dangerous fellow; but I imagined that I was safe to sail with you, since I carry no silver."

"You're as safe as Philemon always was," Glaucon retorted. "I never saw him after he got his goods on shore. Ask my people if he came back to the ship if you don't believe me."

"Oh, I do," I said with perfect truth. Glaucon's rowers, being slaves, could be examined by torture. It was hardly reasonable to suppose that he would put it in their power to give him away.

Glaucon eyed me again with what I thought a threatening look, but he merely grunted. I wondered whether my real uncle would make inquiries if I were lost overboard. I came to the conclusion that Glaucon dared not risk it, but that I should need to be careful ashore in Lemnos and Imbros.

Uneasy though this conversation made me, it had one good result. I could talk of Philemon to the crew and ask them laughingly if I was like him. My purpose in making this voyage on the *Dolphin* was to pick up scraps of

information. This could not be done in privacy on shipboard, where everyone rubs shoulders with his fellows.
By making a jest of the matter, however, I discovered
that they all knew Philemon well. He had proved himself a useful man in a storm which had nearly dashed
them against the rocks of Mount Athos early last season.
They liked him, therefore, and had been aware that his
last cargo was exceedingly valuable. He had not needed
to display it for sale in Byzantium because the merchant
who had bespoken it sent porters to the ship on its arrival. Philemon had dined with him to clinch the bar-
gain. He never returned.

This was all that I had learned when we reached Lemnos. We beached the ship there for the purpose of landing and cooking a meal. Glaucon, like all sailors, had
connections in every port. He went into the town. The
slaves remained on the beach, glad to be able to stretch
their limbs as they pleased and by their presence discour-
aging marauders. I stayed with them, preferring their
company to that of Glaucon, but I did not learn any
more. The fact was, these were simple fellows, not encouraged to think and not enterprising enough to earn
their freedom by deserting, which they surely could have
done in the wilder regions of the Black Sea lands or
Thrace. Perhaps in their dull way they were in love with
the sea, so blue, so purple, pale green, or sulky gray, or
shimmering with light. Perhaps inarticulate feelings
had been stirred by the wind and the stars, the rose-red
cliffs of islands which seemed to float on the water,

schools of dolphins at play around the prow, the sucking and slapping of water endlessly moving. Even more probably they simply liked the life — hard work, poor fare, cramped quarters, but peaceful nights rocked in the swell with the helmsman on watch or round campfires ashore. There was informality between captain and crew, while my father Philemon had been merely a good seaman to them and as such an equal. They had accepted him, but did not regret him. Sailors were often shipwrecked, drowned, stabbed in the back in a foreign port. Sailors absconded, being restless, roving men, here today and gone tomorrow. The crew of the *Dolphin* had shrugged their shoulders over Philemon's whereabouts. It did not concern them.

I switched my attention to Glaucon again, but though I probed as nearly as I dared, I could not make him out. He was, as the barber said, careful. He answered questions with a grunt and kept his mouth closed. Though I watched him, I did not think he had the silver on the *Dolphin*. I wore an amulet which my father had brought home many years ago for me, and I dropped this in a chink among the cargo. Then I rummaged the ship from stem to stern to look for it. Glaucon paid no attention at all, yet had he actually concealed his treasure somewhere, he must have watched me when I searched close to it — or so I thought.

I gave up at last and concentrated on learning the landmarks a pilot must know, the bays we went into, the rocks we avoided, the manipulation of the two big steer-

ing oars, in short the alphabet of the trade which should
have been mine. The flood of my questions appeared to
amuse Glaucon, but he answered readily though briefly,
relaxing his guard.

I retrieved my amulet after sufficient fuss and hung it
on my neck. He took a look at it and said in his slow
way, "Egyptian?"

I nodded, pleased that he himself had started a subject.
He nodded, too, more slowly in agreement. "Thought so.
Theophilos used to deal in those long ago. He likes a
rarity."

I felt my heart leap. Theophilos was the merchant
who had bought my father's perfumes and paid him in
silver. Already I had wondered if this merchant had
some understanding with Glaucon. "Theophilos, eh?"
I said, trying to be casual. "Who's he?"

Glaucon grunted.

"Wait a minute!" I pretended to think. "Theophilos?
Surely . . . Was not Theophilos the man to whom your
friend Philemon sold his cargo for a great sum?"

Glaucon grunted.

I was not to be put off. "Is this Theophilos of good reputation? If not, I would have imagined he might have
questions to answer if ever Philemon had friends to make
inquiries."

He unlocked his lips very briefly. "He's well known."
There was a silence. "He does take risks," Glaucon
added, "dealing in rarities."

"You mean he's a gambler," I pressed. "Win or lose a great sum?"

Glaucon grunted.

Apart from this conversation, if it had value, I learned nothing more through the whole of the five-day voyage. I continued to keep up the pretense of being nephew to the Byzantine and plied Glaucon with questions which he grunted at and finally put a stop to by remarking that he would have imagined that my father would have told me some things before I set out. I desisted, not caring to be unmasked at present, but determined to introduce myself to Theophilos as Philemon's son. He could hardly refuse to see me, for one thing. Besides, I intended to go to the magistrates and, being Athenian, force them to make inquiries. My poor friends the rowers, and some of the servants of Theophilos might be put to the torture. A conspiracy, such as I suspected now, would leave its traces. It was not probable that either Theophilos or Glaucon had risked the killing in person. There would be a desperado hired for that deed.

I went ashore with these thoughts in mind, and within an hour was quite at a loss. Theophilos himself was more impressive a man than I had expected to find him. His house, for one thing, was luxurious beyond the range of common living in Athens. It rather ressembled the Asiatics in its love of display, its walls decorated with frescoes, its floors of marble, and a fountain in its court — this last a convenience which I had never seen in a private household. It seemed incredible that a man with such resources should murder Philemon for the sake of recovering from him two talents of silver.

Theophilos welcomed me with open surprise, explaining that Philemon had only spoken to him of a daughter. "You carry your origin in your face, however," he smiled very easily and with no sign of dismay. "The likeness is striking."

I hardly knew how to proceed. I had been offered refreshment and was pressed to stay and dine. I made my excuses with a certain clumsiness, preferring as I said to waste no time in laying information before the authorities that a crime had been committed.

He smiled again and doubted this. "I made my own inquiries, for Philemon was a friend of mine. Besides, there was a rumor — which proved untrue — that he had not been met with after he dined with me. I can disprove this. There is, too, the disappearance of the . . . woman."

"Who was this woman?"

"A lodging-house keeper of a low class. She had been friends with Philemon for many years, I think. She sold information; he bought it. They were, one might say, in partnership. You realize a trader needs eyes and ears in every port, and sometimes he finds them in places which he does not talk about when he comes home. At all events, such a woman does not leave house and livelihood for a whim. She might be tempted by so large a fortune as two talents of silver."

I considered this proposition bleakly. If Theophilos
had made inquiries, he would be efficient. Could the
magistrates do more? They would have to try. I remem-
bered suddenly a question I had wanted to ask. "Why
did you not pay Philemon by banker's draft as is usual?
He could have exchanged it for the corn he came to buy
and never have needed to carry the silver himself, a
temptation to robbers."

He smiled that ready smile and shook his head. "I
paid Philemon silver because he asked for it. He never
said why, but that was not his way. I thought nothing
of it."

This was the most probable answer. I got up to take
my leave. "You'll not be able to lay your information at
this hour," he pointed out. "The courts are sitting. When
they rise, you may find the magistrates in the Town
House."

I thanked him and said I would spend the time making inquiries on the waterfront, where Philemon must
have been well known. He smiled again. "You might
do worse, and yet you might do better. My own people
have combed the waterfront already, discovering nothing
save that a trader put out at dawn next day, a Cretan who
has not reappeared. A man called Lycon, however, a
neighbor of that woman I spoke of, claims to have seen
her go down the street with someone late that night. He
picked up an amulet which her companion dropped in
the dark — the mate of yours."

I was suddenly excited. "Our tokens were a pair, save

that Philemon's had a little nick in the edge I'd recognize. Either this Lycon has himself murdered Philemon, or else he knows who did."

He shook his head at that. "I know no reason why Lycon should come forward if he were guilty. He must have been aware that some suspicion would be bound to rest on him, the more so because he is by profession an old-clothes man. Such people always have connections with cloak stealers. Their reputation is shady. Had Lycon even suspected crime, he would in prudence have held his tongue."

"You might have told me at once about this Lycon instead of pressing me to dine with you and put off my inquiries."

He was very smooth. "Indeed I might have; but to tell you the truth, I did not wish to involve you in a scrape in a strange town. It's broad daylight to be sure, but — well, you are so young!" He smiled at me again. "I could send a slave with you, but men such as Lycon are suspicious of being pressed. He might deny the whole story."

I would have been glad of the escort, if only for the reason that Glaucon had followed me through the town. He had every right to do so if he had business of his own in this direction, but the thought of his waiting outside almost induced me to appeal for help. However, I did not like the way Theophilos had smiled over my youth. He smiled too often. I said nothing.

"Tell Lycon I sent you," Theophilos continued after a

pause. "I paid him well for this tale, and he'll repeat it if he sees money in it. Offer him five drachmas, no more. Don't let him see how much you carry."

I took my leave of Theophilos, promising to report progress, and I went out into the street. Glaucon was gone. I could not be mistaken, for this was a mere alley, faced by the blank, windowless walls of private houses and frequented only by people who used it as a short cut on their way from the gate of the town to the public market. In such traffic, the size of Glaucon would have made him too conspicuous to be missed. Relieved, I threaded my way towards the market, which I needs must cross to be at the district where Lycon practiced his trade. I had plenty to think over. Notwithstanding what Theophilos had said, I thought it probable that Lycon at least knew the murderer of Philemon. In fact, had the magistrates been induced to make inquiries, it seemed likely that the mystery would have been already solved. For this interview, therefore, I would need to keep my wits about me and not be tempted off the street into any building.

I did not need to take any such risk. Byzantium is a fair city, though not so fair as Athens, nor so large. But being at one and the same time city and port, its working quarters are filthier and more haphazard, crowded as far as possible round the harbor. At least the Piraeus, thanks to Pericles, is laid out in straight lines. The lanes of Byzantium wind in extraordinary zigzags, narrowing in one place to a width in which two can scarcely pass, then suddenly widening into what might have been a tiny square, had not every inch of it been taken up by booths of mud or wattle, clinging crookedly to the outer walls of houses, and each serving as shop and dwelling place for its owner, and often for a woman and a horde of children as well. It was in one of these booths that I found Lycon, a mere open alcove on the street corner, furnished chiefly with a dusty pot or two, a stool, and a chest, presumably containing Lycon's better wares. The chief part of his stock-in-trade, ragged cloaks and well-worn tunics, hung from pegs across the back by an arrangement which prevented them being snatched by passers-by. As for Lycon himself, he was a sallow, hungry-looking man with a leg which had been broken and had not mended well. It was shorter than the other and had twisted his body sideways. He peered up at me, his neck crooked, and began a singsong chant. "Good money, good money for your old clothes. Good clothes for sale cheap. Good money, good money . . ."

I had five drachmas ready in my hand. The rest of my money was in a bag about my waist beneath my tunic. "Theophilos sent me to you." I halted in the opening. "About the merchant Philemon."

It was startling to see the man cringe. If he had not known earlier that Philemon was suspected to be dead, at least he knew now. I clinched it for him. "Philemon the *Athenian*," I told him.

He glared at me in a surly way. "Trades from the Piraeus, but no more Athenian than you or I."

"He was Athenian," I said, "and I can prove it, being his only son by the sister of Cratippos."

If looks could kill, he would have murdered me then. He knew an Athenian would not be suffered to vanish without more inquiries if his kindred chose to press them. However, he tried to carry things off. "Makes no difference to me."

"Why should it?" I agreed. "I come but to offer you money for a token which is said to be my father's. I'll give you two drachmas."

"Ten," he said mechanically. "How did you get here?"

I chose to misunderstand this. "I shipped with Glaucon. Well, three drachmas, then."

"Nine, nine! With Glaucon, that dog! Beware of him. Well, eight then."

"I'll give you four, but that's my last word. As for Glaucon, he's not in my confidence, and nor are you. I'll tell the magistrates what I know and what I guess. I say, four!"

"I'm a poor man and a cripple," he whined. "Seven, eh, for pity's sake!"

"Five for the token and your story as well. You will have to repeat it to the magistrates in any case. Be sure it's the truth."

He spat. "Then six."

I let the money jingle in my hand, pleased with my mastery of the situation. "I say five."

He gave way sulkily. "Then look for yourself. It's in the chest."

I had promised myself not to enter any building, but this booth was only a few feet deep. As I stood in the entrance, passers actually jostled me in the street. Even prudence could hardly forbid me to advance a couple of steps. I lifted the lid.

This chest was full of old clothes, as I had surmised; but in one corner was a bag which seemed to contain the various trinkets Lycon had picked up in the practice of his profession. I bent forward to put out my hand for it. As I did so, Lycon fell on me from behind, his hands at my throat.

It was quickly, skillfully done. Men were actually walking two yards away down the open street. Lycon's only protection for a second or two was the darkness of shadow after the dazzling sun. At the back of his alcove was a little recess behind the clothes into which he tumbled with me out of sight. I felt a roaring in my ears as his thumbs found the point to press. A second later I came dizzily back to my senses. The fingers had slackened; and somebody at the entrance was inquiring, "Where has he gone?"

I tried to call out, but my voice would not obey me. The man was still on me, and I was too bemused to thrash about. Feebly I put up my hand in a pushing gesture which by the favor of the goddess Fortune herself met his arm already descending with a knife. I was scored from elbow to shoulder for my pains, but the wound forced out of my tortured throat a mewling cry like a newborn baby's. In another instant, someone else was on top of us; and we were struggling in a tangled mass of old clothes on the floor. Vaguely I was conscious of commotion, as several people called out. Someone clouted me on the head and said, "Let go, you fool. We want him alive."

I gasped and looked up at Glaucon. My voice was scratchy but appeared to work more or less. "He tried to kill me."

Glaucon grunted in his usual way. "Why didn't you go to the magistrates at once?"

"Theophilos said . . ."

"This fellow will tell us about Theophilos," Glaucon remarked. "I suppose he needed the money more than we thought. I told you that he was a gambler."

"You mean Theophilos?"

"He never knew Philemon had a son," Glaucon said. "Thought he'd stifle inquiries. I didn't dare make 'em myself, being under suspicion. No knowing what evidence he'd have turned up for a small bribe. . . . When you came straight to him, informing him, doubtless, that I did not suspect who you were, he saw his chance. Not easy to trust his own slaves and doorman, but this Lycon must kill you for his own sake. As you saw, he had the skill."

"An expert," I agreed. I was feeling my throat.

"Go to the magistrates," said Glaucon. "I and these good fellows will look after Lycon for you." I got to my feet, starting to mop at my wounded arm.

"Make him tell you where my father lies. I'll throw a

handful of dust into the harbor and say a prayer. I'll not let Philemon wander up and down the banks of Styx with the unburied dead. I wish I had known him."

Glaucon grunted.

"Fools to murder an Athenian," I said. "Perhaps they did not know he really was one. They are mostly aliens in this trade, and no doubt many boast. And for two talents?"

"Who told you it was only two talents?" Glaucon said. "Your father borrowed that sum from Sosias, but I think he intended to make his fortune this time. He was telling me your sister needed a dowry."

"She'll have to wait for that," I said, "until I earn it myself. It will be more modest than my father intended, perhaps, but yet sufficient to marry her to a decent tradesman or a merchant."

Glaucon grunted.

# The Death of the Golden Age

## The Peloponnesian War 430–399 B.C.

# Out of Date

## Athens 430

"You're getting old, Pericles. You're out of date," his nephew said, crossing his legs in a lounging fashion which would not have been tolerated in a young man a few years ago. But in whatever he did, Alcibiades looked so handsome that people forgave his insolent ways. Even Pericles half smiled as he fingered his beard, which was by now white.

"You think you're clever, Alcibiades, don't you? Socrates teaches you the art of puzzling people with innocent-looking questions. You like to use it to ridicule conventional beliefs and pretend you have none of your own. But let me tell you, when we were young, we were just as smart as you, and . . ."

"Oh, Pericles!" The young man clasped his hands in mock enthusiasm. "*How* I wish I had known you when you were at your smartest . . . long ago!"

It was really impossible not to laugh, and yet Pericles was distressed. "No, seriously, Alcibiades, I cannot make you out. You run after Socrates, who claims to be a teacher and a lover of virtue. You shared a tent with him on campaign last summer and came home, I may say, with a crown of valor. Yet your noisy parties, your display, your temper, your insolence is a scandal. When I was busy over the accounts that I must render to the people, you openly commented that if I spent my efforts in wriggling out of presenting accounts at all, I'd be much better off. This sort of thing might pass as a joke, but you behave as if you meant it."

"Oh, I did, uncle, let me assure you." Alcibiades yawned. "I beg your pardon. I was up last night till almost cock-crow. There was a party which began at Lycophron's. About midnight, we took the flute girls and the jugglers and the rest and poured out singing into the streets to liven up other people. It chanced old Hipponicos was giving a party — very staid and grave indeed, no one under fifty. You should have seen his expression when we trouped in! Lycophron bet me I would not have the courage to strike Hipponicos and teach him not to look sour. You wouldn't have me refuse a dare, I hope, uncle, even though Hipponicos is a connection of yours as the first husband of . . . well, your first wife."

Pericles was indeed getting old. If he had been younger, he might have perceived that Alcibiades was by no means at his ease and that he had dragged in this old, unhappy marriage to divert attention from his own inexcusable behavior. It was unheard of for a young man not yet in his twenties to insult a man over sixty, let alone strike him. Such things were never done. Literally too shocked for speech, Pericles took refuge in a dignified and ominous silence which he had the power to make imposing. Indeed, his nephew, who had been subjected to this treatment before, was apt to complain in lighter moments that Pericles was entirely too like Zeus. By just sitting and frowning, he could make one shake in his sandals.

"I went to Hipponicos this morning," he heard himself saying, "and apologized to him humbly, telling him he could beat me if he chose, for I had deserved it."

"And Hipponicos?" Pericles was still very grim.

"Oh, he forgave me freely. We're excellent friends." His confession over, the young man reverted to flippancy again. "I've a way with me, uncle. No one stays angry with me for very long, unless it be you."

"I feel responsible for you," Pericles said heavily. "After all you were of my bringing up." He sighed. "I am not successful, it seems, at educating young men."

"Oh, Xanthippos and Paralos are fools," said the young

man hotly. "You did for them all that was best. Think
nothing of it, uncle. Men have had stupid sons before
and will again. Did you know Xanthippos complains
about how you spend your time . . . you, who never
dine out and think of nothing but the public business?
Xanthippos is telling everybody you wasted a whole day
with his teacher Protagoras at the time when Epitimos
was killed by accident in the games at the javelin throwing. You argued all day, so Xanthippos says, as to
whether the javelin or the man who threw it or the judges
of the games were really responsible. It actually is a nice
point, but your Xanthippos is too dense to see how he's
making a fool of himself."

Pericles shook his head sadly. Part of the attraction
about Alcibiades was his genuine warmth. His own two
older sons were cold and selfish. Their quarrel with him
was simply the fact that he would not increase their al-
lowances, never having stooped to take a bribe or make a
penny out of his services to the Athenian people. The
pity of it was that his youngest son, Aspasia's child, was
not an Athenian because of his foreign mother.

"You are right, I suppose, Alcibiades," he agreed sadly.
"I am old and at a loss. Long ago we criticized our elders
as you do now, and I daresay we puzzled them. We at
least, however, were concerned with what we ourselves
believed in. You are satisfied with making older men
look silly. You believe in nothing."

Alcibiades uncrossed his legs and smoothed his tunic,
which was another source of scandal in itself. Woolen

materials were not good enough for Alcibiades, who must wear fine linen, elaborately pleated and too transparent to be thought decent. The Athenians, though they exercised quite naked, were actually shocked.

"You see," he ran his finger down the pleats, "it's like this, uncle. You believed in too many things . . . Democracy, Freedom, Honesty, Intellectual Truth, even the gods. You've used them all up and left nothing for us. Take democracy, for instance. D'you think we want to spend our lives kowtowing to the ignorant herd as you have done? Are we going to allow them to prosecute our friends on frivolous charges, men like Anaxagoras and Pheidias, or one day perhaps even Socrates? Take honesty. Everyone accepts bribes nowadays but Pericles. The gods? Those crude old stories! Can anyone who saw Euripides's *Medea* feel as you used to feel about the heroes?"

"Sophocles can."

"Oh, Sophocles, yes. He's your age. He makes the gods and heroes plausible by sheer poetic magic. Frankly, when his spell wears off, there's nothing in them."

"Times change so fast!" Pericles was indeed looking old. Even in the quiet half-light of the cool room where they sat, there were sagging lines under his eyes; and the hair had receded from that vast, impressive dome, making it more top-heavy than ever. But the eyes themselves were as calm and compelling as they had always been, giving the impression of an inner strength not to be worn out. "Well, what do you believe in?"

"This present war," said the young man surprisingly. "Our war with the Peloponnesians and Sparta."

"I . . . don't understand," said the older man, puzzled. "War's not a belief. If you mean that this war was bound to come — I have foreseen it for years. I have prepared for it. Athens and Sparta are at opposite poles and cannot rule the Greek world as equals. Sooner or later a struggle must have come. I chose the moment when I was not too old to give it direction."

"You should have left it alone." Alcibiades leaned forward. "I believe in a war, but not your war. Oh yes, we shall win it, but not by your methods. Forgive me, uncle, but you have no genius for war. You're too cautious."

"And you're too rash." Pericles smiled. "Nothing like experience of command to teach a man prudence."

"And so we sit here inside our walls, defending Athens, the Piraeus, and the roads between, while the Peloponnesians are wrecking our farmland and burning our buildings almost in plain sight. We can actually see the smoke rising, and we do nothing."

"They have sixty thousand men, and we half the number. Our strength is on the sea, in our wealth and our trade. They have not the resources to face a long war, nor the mobility to wage one where they please. We shall wear them down."

Alcibiades merely shrugged. "Is that worth doing simply that we may go on in the way we went before? Have you taken a look at your sovereign people, uncle, since they have gathered perforce inside our walls. Have you noticed these sweaty little farmers breathing garlic, men whose superstitions our very grandfathers had grown out of? Have you taken a walk to the Piraeus to see your lords and masters camped in makeshift shacks along the walls on either side of the road? Have you smelled the stink of them and seen their flies? Why, even the rats are finding their quarters too noisome and are dying off in droves. For such people do you intend to master Greece? War should beget change, bring the best men to the top. That's what I believe in."

"You'll change your mind about the people," Pericles insisted. "You're bound to change."

"You think my character's not formed yet?"

"I hope it isn't."

Their eyes met in humorous understanding. Both laughed. The little wrinkles at the corners of Pericles's eyes gave him an expression less lofty, more worldly wise than was usual with him. As for Alcibiades, he looked like the young god of love in a mischievous mood.

"I should like to imagine," Pericles said, "that one day you'll grow out of your antics. Don't disillusion me."

"I'm young enough for a few more," Alcibiades retorted. "Let me see, what shall I do next?"

"Spare me, I beg." They both laughed again. Alcibiades got up.

"I'll be gone then, and leave you in suspense. Till our next meeting . . ." He strolled out, whistling in an improper way, and informed his familiars that the old man cut up quite rough about Hipponicos, but was easily

smoothed down if one knew how to do it. "Too much
on his mind to be bothered if he can avoid it. He's worried about criticism of the war. He knows it's mismanaged."

Pericles, meanwhile, in his deliberate way went out to
pay calls. It was the hour at which people were to be
found in the market place or shops adjacent. The
Painted Portico, adorned with glowing frescoes of the
Battle of Marathon and the Sack of Troy, was crowded
with people who amounted to something in Athenian so-
ciety, all gossiping, bargaining, buying, or doing business. Among these, Pericles moved, exchanging greetings. Unable so much as to stir from his house without
being noticed or to speak to a friend without being suspected of a political motive, Pericles yet understood how
to reach his objectives by none-too-obvious steps. Surprisingly, however, on this occasion a word here and a glance
there betrayed what was on his mind. News went buzzing up and down the Painted Portico and through the
market. "A naval expedition to pay out those Peloponnesians, tit for tat. He'll lead it himself." People nodded
with angry satisfaction, for even in the depths of the
fish market a selective nose could occasionally identify a
whiff of smoke amid the racy smells the place afforded.
Smoke might have come in fact from kiln or smithy; but
at the moment it brought to mind burning olive, blazing
patches of wheat, falling buildings, and the good Attic
land all blackened and bare. Last year when the Peloponnesians had done their worst and retired, men had

gone out to their ruined farms and had wept. All the same, they had toiled to rebuild cottages, replant their vegetable plots, and plow their land. Now the second year of devastation had come, and men were beyond weeping. Some were savage, some despairing. Most still desired revenge, and only a few blamed Pericles because this war had come upon them.

A certain Charicles, a noisy, low-class fellow, too lazy to replant his farm, too old for military service, had drifted into town last year and had scraped a living by hiring out his slave as porter in the market, acting as juryman, sponging on relations, and other more dubious means, while gaining a reputation as a loud- and foul-mouthed democrat of the extreme sort. This Charicles began to follow Pericles at a distance through the crowd, and as he did so, he lifted his voice in an insolent song which one of the comic poets had written concerning the outbreak of war. It chanced that Aspasia, who had lived in Megara long ago, still owned a house there which was rented to one of her freed slaves. When war had started, the Megarians had taken over this place and broken up the establishment. From this incident, the poet had constructed a ribald song, explaining the cause of the war as Pericles's resentment because some Megarians when drunk had carried off slaves of his wife. This song Charicles began to bellow now. Nobody joined him, but nobody on the other hand attempted to stop him. Athenian manners were free. If Pericles objected to the way a fellow citizen amused himself, let

Pericles see to it. Some worthy citizens even grinned
quite openly at the situation.

For all the notice Pericles took, he might not have
heard. Not so the Athenians, who began to nudge one
another and laugh, emboldening Charicles to imitate
Pericles's walk and to enliven the verses of his song by
witty asides of his own or by extra verses of a very lewd
description contributed by some tavern wag. Friends of
Pericles began to bite their lips and look annoyed. One
or two as opportunity offered murmured in Pericles's ear,
but without effect. He continued obstinately deaf and

bland. It was not easy for anyone else to intervene, since Charicles was soon surrounded by a little group who liked the fun and perhaps enjoyed seeing Pericles reviled.

Without any hurry or fuss, Pericles left the portico and made his way to the City Hall, followed by Charicles and a trail of sightseers. He disappeared inside and was thought to have gone to earth rather neatly. The meetings of the Council were public, it is true; but none spoke at them uninvited, save Pericles himself and his colleagues, the generals. He might have had business with the Standing Committee about the arrangements for this proposed expedition. He might merely be taking refuge in the City Hall from insult. In any case, it was not likely that he would emerge before Charicles had grown tired of his jest and gone away.

"Little does he know me," Charicles boasted to his audience. "You wait and see!"

But the audience had business of its own. It melted away, even while Charicles was folding his arms on his chest and heroically vowing to wait till dark if need be. Business in the market was more or less over by noon, so that even Charicles was considering changing his mind and slinking away when, quite unhurriedly and alone as he had gone in, Pericles emerged.

The chance was too good to be missed; and Charicles, who had not been afraid to raise his voice in the crowded market, was not deterred by an almost empty square. He fell into line and started again with full voice, pleased to discover that people came to the doors of their shops

or popped heads out of upstairs windows which over-
looked the street. Some laughed; some even applauded.
Many followed to see what Pericles would do. Once
more, nobody interfered with a free citizen's harmless
pursuit.

Pericles trailed halfway across town, by which time the
latest sensation was known all through the city. When
he disappeared once more into the house of a fellow general, Athens buzzed with the story that the new expedition was to be discussed. In actual fact, Callipos, the general in question, was protesting in some confusion. He
had heard rumors, but being a man of fixed ideas and
small information, he had thought them garbled. "Last
month you desired us to put down the revolt in the
North before we troubled ourselves with the Peloponnesians."

"Unless discontent swelled dangerously in the city."

"Ah yes, to be sure . . . that fellow in the street?"
There was interrogation in the tone if not the words.

"My nephew Alcibiades informed me this morning
that the war is being mismanaged."

"That rascal!" Callippos was surprised enough to criti-
cize, which was not usual. Pericles was twenty years his
senior and in his eyes almost godlike, yet he found himself saying, "I should not have supposed Alcibiades knew
or cared what the people thought."

"He imagines he does not." Pericles smiled. "Alcibiades follows fashion. When fashionable opinions precisely agree with those of the ignorant, then let poli-

ticians take warning. Luckily this vulgar fellow has followed me with abuse all day, attracting great attention to my comings and goings. I have set rumors buzzing so that many may feel more content with the prospect of action."

Callippos laughed. "Here your friends have been wringing their hands over this open insult to you in the public streets, while you have been using the fellow for your own purposes. Who was it, Pericles, who complained that you knew how to look as though you had won, even when defeated?"

"It was Thucydides, the son of Melesias." Pericles looked serious. "And that reminds me, his namesake, the younger Thucydides, was with me yesterday about the sickness which is spreading in the Piraeus. He has visited Hippocrates, as you may know, and shows much interest in medical science. I did not like what Thucydides told me."

Callippos shrugged. "The gods bring sickness, and then they take it away. There are always diseases in the Piraeus brought by sailors. An extra sacrifice or two, a purification perhaps, and they fade out again after some weeks."

"Did you know there were ten people found in one house, all dead or dying? Did you know that plague was spreading in the crowded shacks and tents of our refugee farmers? Did you know that no one is said to have caught it and lived? So Thucydides tells me."

"There should be a public sacrifice to reassure the people." Callippos was only concerned with the political effects of a sickness which his imagination did not present to him as a serious menace.

"I shall arrange it." Pericles felt tired. His old skill at managing people seemed to have deserted him. He knew the methods by which he might make his colleague think that a notion was his own, but the process seemed tedious. Besides, what use to open his mind to Callippos or to tell him that it was not the complaints of Alcibiades and the abuse of Charicles that had chiefly disturbed him. It was the knowledge that, in weighing the resources of Athens for this war, he had never counted on a plague. It was not the discontent today, but the thought of what might follow if the people began to die in thousands. It was Pericles's conviction, implanted by Anaxagoras long ago, that mere processions and sacrifices would not avail to heal a sickness.

He sighed. No use to worry Callippos, whose religion was conventional. Why was it that the very young were talented enough, but would follow no leader, whereas the middle-aged left all their problems to Pericles for solution? Had the fierce energy of Athens drained off the vitality of that generation? So many had died, and now war or plague would kill more. He passed a hand across his high, bald forehead in a fumbling gesture, foreign to him.

"I shall go to the Acropolis," he said, "and speak to the priests of Athene. Sacrifices will reassure the people for a time."

"Just so," Callippos agreed. "There should be a special offering to Apollo likewise, and . . ." he went into details, showing far more animation over religion than he had over his duties as a general. Pericles listened with the special courtesy he reserved for the enthusiasms of other people, but his interest did not extend to the point of making suggestions or prolonging the discussion. Rather when Callippos ran out of ideas, he once more cautiously unburdened himself.

"Do you remember that it was a year ago that Pheidias died? I blame myself for not having sent him a warning."

There had been a special friendship between Pericles and the great sculptor which Callippos had not shared. Indeed, if the truth were told, he thought of Pheidias as a very good sort of fellow, a superior workman. This opinion, however, did not interfere in the least with his admiration for the wonderful works of art Pheidias created. Polite, therefore, in his turn, he deplored the city's loss. "Six years Pheidias had lived in Elis, had he not? He had made them the gold and ivory Zeus with which no image in the world can compare, save our own Athene. Who would have imagined that the Eleans would put him to death for no better reason than being Athenian?"

"I should have thought of it myself. I knew this war would be bitter."

"He would not have believed you."

Pericles looked at him, surprised at such chance per-

ception. "You are right, Callippos. He would not have.
Pheidias was of all men I ever knew the largest-minded
and the least suspicious of others. Well, since I must go
to the temple, I will look at our Athene again and see the
portrait of himself which Pheidias made in the midst of
the battle scene on her shield. He set me beside him
there, to protect him as he said. Alas, I could not do it."

Callippos frowned. "That piece of sacrilege more than
any other thing brought Pheidias's exile about. To carve
living people on the very shield of the goddess! What
possessed him?"

Pericles did not answer this, for the intimate secrets of
his friendship were too precious to confide to any mere
colleague. He got up to take his leave, remarking that
his follower in the street must be getting tired of waiting.
Privately he might hope that Charicles had left him, but
his manner was perfectly easy and unconcerned. If it
added to his burdens to be insulted in the open street, he
would not say so.

Charicles, as it chanced, was busy partaking of the re-
wards of enterprise in the nearest tavern. Several cronies
of the extreme radical sort were dispensing drinks and
sharpening their wits with lewd suggestions. They had
posted a boy in the street to watch for Pericles, but were
unwilling to leave their wine half drunk and their song
unfinished. Thus by the time they came up with him, he
was already ascending the steps of the beautiful entrance
porch to the Acropolis, which he himself had caused to
be constructed. There was nothing for it but to wait till

he came down, since the Acropolis was far too holy a
place for their ribald behavior.

It was late afternoon. Pericles, who had taken refreshment with Callippos, would dine late. His wants were
simple. In the meantime, he went into the Parthenon,
feeling as he always felt beneath the undying beauty of
the statues on that building as though the gods themselves sat overhead. He had often questioned in his
mind who the gods were and whether their natures, their
names, and their legends were really of the kind men
thought they were. Yet the poetry and the art of that
great age which he had known how to harmonize all
told him with one voice not to inquire. It did not matter.
For not by name and by legend, but by greatness of
spirit alone was the godhead understood. Alas, to
Socrates, Euripides, and the young men, such noble simplicity was out of date. They must tear the gods to pieces
in the hope of finding what lurked behind. Only too often they ended up with nothing to believe in.

Pericles went through the entrance room and into the
heart of the temple where the great Athene stood, her
splendor contrasting with the bare white walls of that
perfect, simple structure. For Athene was white and
gold, one ivory arm extended to support a Victory in her
open palm, one loose by her side, just touching spear
and shield. Her complexion was ivory, too, lips painted,
eyes set with colored stones, cheeks delicate white and
finely carved. All her armor was gold, her triple-crested
helmet, her breastplate with the Gorgon's head, her

204

THE DEATH OF THE GOLDEN AGE

shield and spear. Her long flowing robe was gold
and bright enamel. There were pictures on her shield,
her breastplate, helmet, even on the rims of her sandals;
yet the effect of so much richness was not confusion.
Though gorgeous, Athene was simple; though elaborate,
majestic. One could gaze at her by the hour and never
tire.

There was a quality about this masterpiece of Pheidias
profoundly reassuring. Bitterness, skepticism, war,
plague, death, even defeat, what did they matter once
Pheidias had seen eternal beauty? Sophocles had known
the same vision, and the sovereign people, despite their
turbulence and ambition, had comprehended it. Let
come what would, Athens had seen a golden age. Such
thoughts did not occur specifically to Pericles, whose eyes
as a statesman were still fixed on things ahead. Yet without thinking them out, he felt them. There was an in-
fluence this age of his must needs exert on the future of
government, of religion, above all of Athens. Something
undying had come to pass which would not vanish in a
generation or two. The heavy burden of anxiety and age
which had oppressed Pericles was lifted now. He could
go quietly about his business, speak to the guardians of
the temple, talk of the omens and the anger of Apollo,
say something consoling to a farmer who put himself in
his way, and above all radiate that calm and tempered
optimism with which he had faced war. The imperial
city, with her flexibility, her wealth, her modern ways,
was fitted to govern. The Peloponnesians were not.

Athens must and would win, no matter how the battles went.

Pericles came down from the Acropolis as it grew dark; and he made his way homeward with Charicles on his tail, more drunken and abusive, far less witty, and more offensive even than before. Yet Pericles walked at his usual pace, intent apparently only on getting home before dark, since he had no torchbearer with him. He went calmly into his own house, leaving Charicles in the street. He summoned his slave.

"There is a citizen outside," said Pericles quietly, "who has come with me a long way, and it grows dark. Take your torch and light him home through the streets. I would not wish him to suffer an inconvenience on my account, for he is an Athenian."

# The Head

## Macedonia 406 B.C.

KING ARCHELAOS of Macedonia was in one of his Greek moods. These occasions came round as surely as the spring, when he migrated from his snowbound fortress in the hills to his new Greek capital in the low-lying lands by a navigable river. Up this, Greek ships came sailing in, and King Archelaos flew into a passion if any of his attendant chieftains disgraced him by displaying lack of culture. These were uncomfortable times for the court of Archelaos. It was not that men minded his temper or the bursts of savagery in which he indulged now and then when he felt himself fretted. They respected violence in their prince, but they liked his jollity and his deep carousing very much better than his determination to be a Greek and a civilized man of the world. They despised his architects, his artisans, and his traders as people of no family at all who earned their living by work, did not care for hunting, used coined money, and bored them every day with long discussions. These opinions they were forced to keep to themselves, for Archelaos had a short way with anyone who displeased him, while the increase in wealth and trade was undoubtedly giving him more arbitrary power than his predecessors.

Such being the state of affairs, the court of Archelaos was for the moment impeccably Greek; and the king himself was in high good humor. He had every right to be so, since in his pursuit of culture, he had scored an undeniable coup. He had got a poet. Nor was this just any poet, but an Athenian, in fact the greatest Athenian of all, the awe and wonder of the whole world in which Greek was spoken. Less than ten years earlier, the Athenians had suffered their greatest disaster of the Peloponnesian War, which was at this time still dragging on after twenty-five years. Few of their soldiers had returned home from that campaign, and those that did so had been given their freedom at the price of teaching their captors the latest songs of Euripides. Of Euripides, not of Sophocles, the poet of classic beauty. Of Euripides, the poet of love, of agony and despair, of romance and reason, of all the human aspirations or failures which had followed the golden age of Olympian glory. It was this Euripides that King Archelaos, like a provident spider, had enticed and wrapped in a careful cocoon and stowed in his larder.

To be sure, this poet was old and rather ill. He was a little man, hunched together and moving feebly, subsisting mainly on goats' milk and disconcertingly apt to fall asleep in the midst of a banquet. His hair had vanished except for a fine, silky rim round the edge of his baldness. His beard straggled and was snow-white. For no reason, tears would run down the side of his nose and drip into this beard. He mumbled oddly because he had lost all his teeth. One could scarcely understand him.

None of this mattered to Archelaos, whose idea of conversation was mainly to hear himself talk. This old poet was Euripides himself, wasn't he? No need for him to say much as long as he could still write. Why, this play he had written was as good as ever he wrote. Everybody whom Archelaos had admitted to rehearsals agreed that it was so.

"You like my theater, hey?" the king was saying in his thick, accented Greek. "Stone seats, hey? They're only wood in Athens, aren't they?"

The slow tears started down the old man's cheek at the thought of that beloved wooden theater. He made no answer, but the king's questions were merely rhetorical. Archelaos was shifting himself on his fine cushioned chair with impatience, turning often to peer at the audience still filing in, or summoning attendants to be sure that the actors had everything they wanted.

"Those garlands," he fussed. "Vines not leafed out yet. Had to use ivy. Bacchus has gold leaf. Did they show you his mask?"

The mask of the god Bacchus had not pleased the king. It had had to be altered. Time was when Euripides had seen to all such things himself, had personally instructed the trainer in his music, let no rehearsal take place without his presence, guided the producer in choice of costumes or minor actors, in fact had worn himself out demanding perfection. Here he had not done so. He felt too ill, too unhappy in this exile. The king fussed him. The Greek that was spoken in these parts grated on his ear. He had been thankful to let Archelaos import a professional trainer. The king had added the functions of producer to the already incredible number of his own activities. Archelaos was always restless when not occupied, and the moments of waiting between his own entry into the theater and the appearance of the procession were being considerably prolonged by his messages of interference.

"Just like the festival of Dionysus at Athens," the king said. "Same day, too. Only one play, though. A special festival for Euripides's latest play. A compliment, hey?"

Once more the old man did not answer. He could see far too clearly the dear, familiar scene at Athens — the preliminaries first — the sacrifices, the procession, presentation of tribute from the allies, the touching occasion when the orphan wards of the state were given their weapons. All this he would sit through with quivering nerves, perhaps knowing that Sophocles was on first and that his plays were rumored to be the greatest of all his works. It was aggravation of the poet's sick longing for Athens that this performance took place on the very same day, and that he must remember what would be going on there. King Archelaos was highly pleased with the coincidence which he had contrived. He repeated himself.

"Same day as the festival in Athens, hey? They've not got Euripides this time. A bit cold here in March, hey? But we're all hardy up north. Should be warmer in Athens."

A messenger came to say that all was ready, but was forced to stand on one side while Archelaos boasted of the play to his other neighbor, a chieftain from Thrace named Tereus, who was a cousin.

"Out of compliment to us," the king said. "About the god Bacchus. He came through Macedonia on his way to Greece, and all our women were mad for the new worship. They went dancing and singing on the mountains, possessed by the god. They hunted beasts with their bare hands. This legend's laid in Thebes, but it's the same thing. You'll see how Pentheus, the king, disbelieved in the god, tried to imprison him, put him to death. Bacchus in vengeance had him torn to pieces by the Theban women . . . mad of course and out on their revels, thinking him a beast. Not seeing he was a man till they came to their senses. Sad and terrible."

"No use in tearing beasts to pieces," Tereus replied. "That's no kind of hunting. Ruins the game."

At any other time this uncultured remark might have caused trouble, but luckily the king was not listening at all. He had caught the messenger's eye.

"Well, well. What are they waiting for? Why haven't the flutes started up? Where's that procession?"

The flutes began to play, and presently the procession came filing in through the left-hand side of the entry, round the altar which stood in the middle of the circular dancing place, and out at the right. Since there was but one drama, the procession was not large, which was the reason why Archelaos had not chosen to parade it through the town. However, he had swelled it by garlanded oxen for sacrifice led by slaves, girls carrying trays heaped with flat cakes, little children with baskets of violets for which the hills had been scoured, vast pitchers of wine moving on wheels, in fact the ingredients of a great public feast which was to follow. Furthermore, he had lengthened the program by introducing a traditional war dance performed by groups of young men and a crude acrobatic exhibition by a troupe dressed in goatskins and grotesque masks, representing the half-savage satyrs, the followers of Bacchus.

Between these minor performers paraded the persons of the drama itself, the First Actor, clothed in the gorgeous purple and gold robes of the god Bacchus riding at their head in a chariot drawn by asses and guided by garlands of ivy held by dancing attendants. He wore the Bacchus mask under a high, tiara-like headdress wreathed in gold. The face was youthful, highly colored, and had its red lips open in a great shout of joy so that the words of the actor might ring out through them clear and unmuffled. He was turning from side to side as he rode so that this vivid countenance might be visible to the topmost row of his audience, who might not have seen his uncovered face so clearly. Behind him walked an attendant, displaying the mask and cloak of his minor role, the aged prophet Tiresias, whose function was to warn King Pentheus in vain. After him stalked the Second Actor, King Pentheus himself with dark, distorted, frowning mask and flowing cloak of saffron embroidered with figures in black and worn over an underdress of black and scarlet. His second part, carried behind him, was the king's mother, Agave, a wild woman, frenzied by the power of the god, with flowing hair and ivy garland, mouth distorted and shrieking. Behind Agave . . .

"Who's that?" asked Euripides involuntarily. The next comer was neither masked nor robed, though there was a garland of ivy on his head. He was carrying nothing and seemed white with panic at finding himself where he was. His eyes went rolling from side to side as though, had he dared to, he would have dashed for shelter somewhere and hidden himself.

"Hey, what?" inquired King Archelaos, his gaze still on the Bacchus. "What did you say? Who?" He appeared quite suddenly to take in the question. "Oh, ah, yes. Scenery, hey?"

"What's a scene shifter doing up there," Euripides persisted, "in the middle of the actors?"

This time the king turned to glance at his companion with a curiously dubious eye. "Must have got out of place."

Euripides opened his mouth to say more, but he shut it again. He felt too old and ill to endure one of the king's rages. Better not call attention to imperfections today. He knew that the war dances would be quite interminable and that refreshments in the form of cakes and wine would be pressed on him which his stomach would revolt at. Already he was dizzy with the familiar strain before a performance. No competition came in question today, and yet the anticipation of seeing his poetry clothed in flesh and blood was still an agony. This *Bacchae* had caused him more ecstasy and pain than any of his plays, except one heartbroken one which he did not care to think of.

Luckily, almost at once the king's attention was absorbed by Third Actor in the gorgeous garments of his major part, old Cadmos, the king's wise grandfather, counseling restraint. His other two parts were rustics, a herdsman and a messenger, each bearing stories of the revels of the women in the hills, and the latter describing the death of the king at his own mother's hands.

"That's a Macedonian," Archelaos was saying. "My own discovery. He can speak clear Greek when he chooses, and I told him I'd flog the skin off his back if he disgraced me by dialect today. Oh yes, I've a good ear for accents."

It was not necessary to reply, for now the flute players were piping for the chorus, boys dressed as wild women, comparable to those mutes who pranced around the car of Bacchus. The king was muttering to himself, "Could have brought my lion on here. Why not? Why not? Should have thought of it." He had set his heart on adding a mountain lion to the procession of Bacchus, but the asses of the god's chariot had panicked at it. Besides, the wild beasts which frolicked in the god's train were supposed to run free. Even King Archelaos had thought of no answer to that, but frustration still galled him. It would have gingered the procession up, he felt. Nothing like a sensation!

After the chorus came the trainers and assistants, crowned with golden garlands and draped in heavy cloaks with brilliant borders. On the whole, Euripides thought, the exuberant fancy of the king had suited the richness and wildness of this particular play. Archelaos had spared no effort or expense. The scarlet, saffron, blue, and gold of the costumes were garish, barbaric, oriental. Even the ivy of which he had complained was beribboned with silver, entwined with artificial grapes, and gay with anemones The very goatskins of the herdsmen were snow-white, and the messenger's costume with a flaming disregard for realism was scarlet and green.

Unfortunately, when the play started, the performance seemed less brilliant than the costumes. First Actor, an old professional hired for the purpose, was adequate, and Second Actor might well prove passable, though his singing voice was rough. The Macedonian was agony to hear with his illiterate brogue not quite covered up by overconscious refinement. The chorus was worse. It danced well, to be sure, and had been painstakingly trained in the complex music which Euripides preferred to the old-fashioned chanting. Their enunciation, however, was poor; and the lovely poetry on which he had spent himself was more than half lost. He closed his eyes in despair and tried to let the lines sing in his head. He had not been able to refuse the king's offer of wine during the war dancing; and as he had foreseen, he felt ill. The dull pain in his stomach which tormented him most of the time was growing acute. He twisted himself in his seat, attempting to ease it by change of position.

First and Second Actors brought him to himself. The triumphant, careless god and the puritan king were creating an atmosphere for themselves, an interplay of ideas, a dramatic tension which was carrying the play, despite

the chorus and the deplorable figure of old Cadmus.
There was a hush in the stands, which had been restless.
Euripides let his mind half-wander, carried away by his
own words which meant to him so much — so very
much more than people could imagine. How far could
strangers comprehend? Were they surprised as the story
twisted and turned with the development of the contrast
between the moralist king and the amoral god? Had
they expected Euripides to take an old legend, as he so
often had done, and hold it up to mockery, in effect saying: "If these be gods who do such things, I care for none
of them." Were they disappointed that neither Bacchus
nor the king was right or wrong? Would there be anyone in the stands so subtle as to understand why? For
both of these parts were Euripides himself. Their conflict was his own. It had torn him in pieces. It had shipwrecked him. It had cast him up on this foreign shore,
sick and dizzy with longing for home.

It is hard for a sensitive man to be brought up in a
golden age, not remembering the contrast between these
days and the harsher past. Euripides had never been
complacent. His understanding of his time was deep, but
critical. His deathless poetry came to be loved or re-
sented with almost equal passion by the city which he
held dear. Worst of all, the golden age issued in a long,
grinding war during which a civilized people descended
by degrees to the level of their neighbors. Too late the
poet discovered that the golden age was his own, that the
ideals at which he had unthinkingly whittled away were

his as well. The poet and the moralist in him were now at war. The inspiration of the one and the anger of the other had destroyed him.

It was in the year 416 that the Athenian people, beginning to be desperate, looked around for further allies who might by paying them tribute increase their resources for war. Taking advantage of their supremacy at sea, they began to put pressure on the little island of Melos, which had no importance, wealth, or trade, but perhaps by mere example showed an awkward independence. The Athenians demanded tribute. The men of Melos refused. Then the Athenians, the most enlightened and civilized people the world had known, descended on Melos, enslaved the women and children, and slaughtered the men. Such were the effects of plague and war and the death of Pericles. But in the following spring at the Great Dionysia, nine years ago this day, the poet Euripides reproached his countrymen in a play which he had written with tears and passionate anger. It was the story of how the Greeks took Troy, mercilessly slaughtered the men, and made the women their slaves. Ever since those burning verses of his a deep resentment had been growing between the poet and his beloved city. If only he could have kept silent! If only the inspired god would have let him alone!

It had come to exile at last as the war grew grimmer and harder. Athens fought for her very life and could afford no critics. Even the poet for whom there was no other place in the world seemed an enemy now. All this had been in Euripides's mind as he wrote in compliment to King Archelaos this wild drama about a meddling, moralist king and an inspired god.

He was lost in a dream of his far country. His mind had wandered to the smell of thyme and the murmur of bees, the cave he used to sit in, listening to water splashing as he worked. King Archelaos nudged him. "Sleeping, hey? You can't sleep now. The king's mother comes dancing back from the hills with the chorus, carrying the head of a wild beast in her arms. Then as the frenzy fades out, she recognizes the head of her own son. Sensational, eh?" It was obvious that in his pride as producer, the king had forgotten the author's share. His tone was condescending.

Euripides blinked and looked up, trying to straighten himself at the cost of a pang which almost made him groan. "I'm listening," he protested. "I can sometimes hear better if I don't look at it."

"You ought to see this."

Long ago the poet had made up his mind it was perfectly useless to argue with King Archelaos. It merely provoked him to insist. Much easier to give way. He said resignedly, "I know. I'm looking."

The music of the flutes was very wild. The king's mother Agave was entering with her horde of maddened women. She had the fatal head in her arms and was cradling it in gloating ecstasy. Euripides noticed with a certain disgust that the king's sense of realism had gone beyond the bounds of taste. Agave's dappled fawnskin, her girt-up clothes, even her arms were stained with red dye, as a woman's might be after helping her sisters tear a man to pieces. Loud and clear through the shrieking mask came the voice of Second Actor, uplifted in a harsh song of triumph as she rocked and dandled the head. Behind her, the women tossed arms into the air, plucked flowers from their garlands, tore them into fragments, threw them wildly, unmeaningly, expressing by frantic, purposeless motion the madness brought by the god.

With a fierce, inarticulate cry, Agave seized the head by the hair and held it up for all to see. It was real! Euripides gave a gasp that was almost a groan as something twisted itself inside like a knife in his stomach. It was a man's head and fresh-killed. He could see it drip. Oh Athens, the glorious, the civilized, the far-off! The king nudged him. "Sensation, hey?" King Archelaos grinned in triumph. "Told you that rustic in the procession was scenery, didn't I, hey? Thought I'd surprise you."

Twisting again in his seat, Euripides looked at the king, his features writhing.

"Hey, what's the matter?" Even Archelaos was alarmed. Turning from Agave, who had lifted the bloodstained thing to her lips and was kissing it, he stared full at the poet, slumped in his seat with ghastly face. Archelaos shook him.

"He was only a criminal condemned to death. What's the matter?"

Euripides did not answer. Actually he did not even

hear. He was beside himself with pain, lost in a red mist; but there was a murmuring in his ears which might have been the sound of water beating endlessly on rocks. He was dreaming that he lay in his cave in distant Salamis and let the pain wash through him. He knew he was dreaming; and yet if the pain had its way, he need never wake.

# The Old Juryman

## Athens 399 B.C.

THE MOON had set, but though the sky was faintly gray with dawn, the land was dark. Old Alexis used his staff to feel his way down the public highway, which was merely a dried-up stream bed filled with loose rock. This arrangement, though inconvenient enough in winter and spring when the water was running, made practical sense for the farmers on either side, who had carefully terraced the banks as close to the edge as they dared, protecting their hard-won gardens from flood by walls of rock. Alexis knew their boundaries to the inch. He could reel off the number of olives every farmer had replanted since the war and was proud to be consulted about the stumps of sacred olive trees, which the Peloponnesians had by no means spared when they devastated the land. These useless stumps which must not be grubbed up were a trial to farmers where land was so precious. To make things worse, many owners were no longer sure which they were. Nearly all these plots had changed hands or had descended a generation or two while the war forbade cultivation.

A little owl hooted, flying home to bed. Some hours earlier the night had been noisy with them, but by now it was almost time for the cock. Alexis hobbled as fast as he dared, considering the nature of the ground and his bad leg. He might quite possibly beg a ride part way going home from the charcoal burners, who drove their asses in heavy-laden, but sometimes returned in mellow good-humor if they had a profitable day. If not, well, he would sleep outdoors somewhere, wrapped in his cloak. He could be certain he would not be missed by his son-in-law Cleophon, who had no work for him except at harvest. Vine and olive ripened with the aid of the good gods, and a little plowing sufficed for the grain- and vegetable-growing.

Life had been easier when Alexis was young. His own old father had been many years a burden; but in those days the olives on his farm had been in maturity, heavy with fruit. The three children had been early trained to help, and there had been slaves. All this was now gone.

The elder of his sons had died of the plague in the second year of the war. The younger had taken service with the fleet and had survived there until the last defeat of all, when the Spartans had massacred their prisoners to a man. By that time, Alexis was past looking after himself. Bred a farmer, he had no particular trade. Unskilled labor was performed everywhere by slaves. There was little for a destitute old man to do but to sell his burned-out land for what it would fetch and beg a lodging from Cleophon, his son-in-law and neighbor.

Sparrows were beginning to cheep as Alexis came down from the uplands, emerging onto a genuine road with actual cart tracks cut into the rock or rutted deep into the hard earth. Other people were already on their way into the city. Behind Alexis, a man with a moving load of furze whose massive outline must somewhere under it conceal a donkey was disputing with a citizen bent under a load of strong-smelling goat cheese.

"His trial's today, I tell you," the furze cutter insisted. "And if I had my way, there'd be less fuss about letting bygones alone and more about seeing that good democrats were protected from such people."

"Ah, that was a bad time after the war!" The cheese carrier shook his head. "Everybody was a little crazy then. Besides, the Spartans would have nothing to do with a democracy in Athens. Not," he added in haste, "that I was for the government of the Thirty. I'm a good democrat and always was. Ask anyone. I spit on the memory of Critias." He suited the action to the word. "But our democracy has been restored under the agreement that these past grudges be forgotten. And Critias is dead."

"It was this Socrates, they say," the furze cutter pointed out, "who corrupted Critias by teaching him to despise the gods and the laws. Socrates has ruined many young men. His favorite pupil was Alcibiades, no less."

"Curse Alcibiades," the cheese vendor agreed. "Our defeat was mainly owing to him when all's said and done. Look out, there, old man! My dog'll snap."

"Dogs like me," replied Alexis calmly, letting the creature sniff his hand as he fell back to join the others. "There then! Good dog! Did you know that Socrates was ordered by the Thirty to arrest a citizen at the time when Critias and his friends were getting money by putting wealthy men to death on charges of treason? Socrates and four other men were ordered to make an arrest. If such instructions had been given to you by the Thirty, what would you have done?"

"By Zeus, what I had been told!" The cheese vendor hitched up his basket. "It would have been my life against some other man's. That's why I say the past ought to be forgotten."

"So thought the four other men," Alexis agreed. "But Socrates went quietly home, preferring to disobey, no matter what it cost."

"And well he might," exclaimed the furze cutter, "seeing that Critias was such a friend of his — seeing that Critias's nephews, Adeimantos and that young man they nickname Plato, were and still are his disciples. What risk did he run?"

Alexis shrugged in his turn. "I know nothing of that. The cousin of the wife of the man who was taken was a connection of Cleophon, who married my daughter. Leon was his name."

"You on the jury list?" the furze cutter inquired.

Alexis nodded. "Pay isn't much when you get it, but these times are hard for old men. If only I lived nearer into the city with my bad leg! If I'm not lucky when the lots are drawn, I'll sleep in the open and try again to-morrow. There's a cousin who sometimes spares a bite, but not too often."

"Hold on by the load if you like," the furze cutter said sympathetically. He jerked at the donkey. "Whoa there!"

Alexis wound his hand into the withes with which the bundles were tied. The donkey was prodded with a sharp stick by its owner, who seemed to know how to get at its hide; and the group proceeded.

"What's the size of the jury for Socrates's trial today?" inquired the cheese vendor.

"Five hundred." What with his own stick and the help of the donkey, Alexis was getting along pretty well. "There'll be other juries needed for other trials. I don't know how many."

"You know Socrates?"

"Seen him. I was in the city for most of the war, and you can't miss a man as ugly as that."

"That great flat nose and thick lips! A hideous fellow!"

"It's a warning," the furze cutter proclaimed in solemn tones. "Socrates ought to have been exposed at birth. It never pays to bring up a misshapen baby. I say, it's a warning from the gods that such a child will bring a curse. This Socrates's father was a decent stonemason, and his son was bred to the trade. But it was no use bringing up such a boy as an honest tradesman. His father ought to have known better, mark my words."

"Heard Socrates talk?"

Alexis shook his head. "How should I? He spends his day lounging about the exercise ground or the market, talking to people who are rich enough to have time on their hands. I've got my work cut out to scratch a living."

"I heard him once," the cheese vendor said. "I went on campaign, and there he was. It was very . . . beautiful."

"What about?"

This seemed a difficult question. The cheese vendor scratched his head and hitched his load again and glanced at the horizon, which was gray with early light. "We-ell, in a sort of way he talked about courage."

"How d'you mean, 'in a sort of way'?"

"We-ell, he was saying how courage in war isn't really courage at all."

The furze cutter snorted. "That's just what I mean

about the harm he does. Here you were, sent out to fight battles; and so Socrates starts speaking against courage."

"It wasn't like that, not at all," the cheese vendor protested. "Only I didn't understand very well, and it was long ago. He's seventy now. He made us all feel courage was a glorious thing, but it wasn't what we thought it was. I do remember that."

"That's just what I mean," the furze cutter repeated. "Courage is courage. It's a perfectly simple quality that everyone understands; but Socrates tried to persuade you it was something else. No wonder we lost the war!"

"He fought very well," the cheese vendor protested. "I remember him in the retreat striding along at his own pace with his head in the air, quite coolly surveying the enemy pressing from behind. People were breaking into a run, throwing away their shields, urging each other to get away fast. Socrates would not panic, and a few of us who rallied around him came off safe because the enemy thought it best to leave us alone. Why, you might almost say he preserved our lives."

"And his own, too, curse him," the furze cutter pointed out. "Far better for the city if the enemy had cut him off. How can you expect the gods to favor Athens when disbelievers like Socrates blaspheme?"

"Well, that's to be decided today," Alexis pointed out. "He is accused of impiety, disbelief in the gods, and corrupting our youth. If they prove their case, we'll be rid of Socrates and may see then how we get on without him."

"Mind you vote for death, old man."

"I may not be drawn on the jury," Alexis reminded him.

"And if you are so?"

"Why, he'll wait to see what Socrates says," the cheese vendor snapped. "Won't you, old man?"

Alexis hesitated. These younger men could never perfectly understand how times had changed since he and Socrates were in their prime. One could not talk to them about it. In addition, he prided himself on his upright conduct as a juryman. Old, penniless, and dependent as he was, this office was his sole dignity. It did not become him to judge a case before he had heard it, even if impiety were among the accusations. He compromised by saying, "It is not for us jurymen to fix a penalty if Socrates is condemned. His accusers will propose one, and Socrates must suggest an alternative. We merely vote between them."

"Have it your own way," the furze cutter snapped, annoyed. "Don't come round and ask to ride my donkey home if you don't get rid of him for us."

"You'll see what I mean when you hear Socrates make his defense," the cheese vendor insisted.

They were moving across the plain by now, and the sun rising behind the eastern ridge had turned the sky from gray to a colorless blue. Athens was visible ahead as a wall, a gate, and the Acropolis sharply etched in the clear air. In the adjacent farmlands, goats and people were astir. By various pathways, other rustics were joining the road. Some, like Alexis, were older men who earned a pittance sitting on juries. More brought honey to sell, a hare or two, goatskins, or other produce. The furze cutter, who by nature of his trade came often to Athens, greeted them all, seeming to remember whose wife was sick, whose son was lazy, whose daughter was shortly to be married off to a suitable neighbor. Chatter and repartee arose on the air, in the midst of which the cheese vendor, who had trudged by Alexis in silence for half a mile, said suddenly to him, "I've a brother-in-law among the charcoal burners, old man. If you need a ride homewards and he's out of humor . . ." he nodded at the furze cutter's back, "I could do something for you . . . if the trial goes well." He winked.

Alexis thanked him, really pleased. Owing to the great size of the juries, actual bribes did not come his way; but minor favors gave him a delightful sense of his own importance. Already these rustics, who had no personal connection with Socrates's case, were soliciting his vote. He grasped his staff more firmly in his hand as he limped along, recalling a charm which he always said to himself before drawing lots to bring him luck.

The trial was assigned to the red court, and Alexis was lucky in drawing a red acorn. As he arrived, he found the accusers and their friends drawn up outside. If Socrates had possessed any sort of good sense, he would have been there also with his wife and sons in their shabbiest clothes, imploring the jurymen to save them all. It was almost insulting, in fact, that he was not. Even Socrates's friends on the jury seemed embarrassed. "Socrates is not like other men," said one of these to Alexis. "Being innocent, he will not ask favors which he knows we must give him of right."

"That's all very well," replied Alexis, annoyed, "but he might show good manners and proper respect for the court."

"He doesn't feel respect," put in a sour old man. "We all know who his friends have been."

"That's to be forgotten," the first man protested. "There are good democrats among Socrates's friends as well."

"Such as Alcibiades?"

"If he was taken in by that traitor, so were we all."

"Hallo, Alexis! So you got into town in spite of your bad leg! Sit by me."

"Hallo, Alexis!"

Alexis exchanged greetings, found a good seat, and accepted a handful of nuts in the happy consciousness that his pay would allow him to stand modest treat later on. His leg throbbed painfully; but he was enjoying himself with friends of his own age, many of whom lived in the city as he had done during the war. On jury duty, he caught up with their gossip and relived the past. "There's Demo," he pointed out. "Demo always has to be waked up to give his verdict. A scandal, I call it, that his tribesmen never took him off the jury list."

"He's well connected."

The two old men looked at each other and wagged

their beards in gloomy agreement. "Everything depends on whom you know these days," Alexis sighed. "Not like it used to be . . . Good nuts, these, Dinon, but hard to crack with my old teeth."

"None of us growing younger, eh? Look at Simon, too blind to see and far too deaf to hear. They say he always votes for condemnation."

"He won't this time. Socrates is his wife's cousin."

"Really?"

"Yes, indeed he is. And they say . . ."

"There's Socrates now!"

"Where?" Alexis craned to look. "I hardly know him dressed up in a cloak and with sandals on! Even in winter, Socrates always used to wear a simple tunic."

Dinon brought his gnarled hand down on his thigh in an impatient gesture. "Everybody but Socrates puts on his oldest clothes at his trial to look wretched and to implore our mercy. Socrates makes himself neat as if to say he doesn't care for our verdict. He's laughing, too. Look at him! We'll see about that."

"D'you like this Anytos who put up the accusation? Wasn't too well thought of in the city towards the end of the war."

Dinon pursed his lips. "He's shown himself a good democrat since. He speaks sense at the Assembly. Not like most of these new men. Respects the court, too." They watched Anytos, who was circulating as the jury took their seats, greeting friends and saying a persuasive word or two. Anytos was a fine, upstanding figure of a man; and his manner was hearty. Somehow, Alexis did not regard him with favor. He frowned.

"Young whippersnapper hardly out of his forties! That Meletos who is going round with him looks hardly grown. They'll not remember how it used to be when Socrates was young. Everything was different as long as Pericles lived." Alexis had been thirty-nine when Pericles died; and, rustic though he was, the golden age had meant something to him — unhappily he did not know what. He could only shake his head, reflecting that Anytos could never have been bathed in the brilliant light of those times, unless in childhood. How should young Meletos understand the life of a Socrates? Vaguely Alexis felt uneasy; but he was not accustomed to complicated thinking and merely was conscious that men of his generation ought to stick together. "Young whippersnapper!" he repeated, seeking to convey his meaning merely by raising his voice. Communicated in such an imperfect fashion, however, his feelings obtained no sympathy.

"Anytos is old enough to know very well why the war went wrong. Meletos has listened to Socrates, which is more than you ever did, I'll wager, Alexis. He heard Socrates teach other young men to laugh at morality and at religion, too. It was a game with Socrates to make fun of older people by tangling them in arguments until they got confused. He never respected . . ."

His other neighbor nudged Dinon sharply for silence. The water clock which timed the speeches had been filled. The various supporters of accusers or accused had taken their places. The clerk of the court had his pile of papers beside him. Nothing was wanting but that the jury should subside and the opening ceremonies of the trial should begin. Alexis duly tried to attend. He felt, however, as though he had been interrupted in discussing a point which was all-important. He did not know what this was, but he hoped uneasily that Socrates or his accusers would explain it.

Several hours later, Alexis had almost forgotten his doubt. If Socrates had indeed defended the golden age, or even himself, his manner of doing so had been unusual. Anytos, as a politician should, spoke good horse sense. His colleague Meletos was frankly emotional. As for Socrates — well, what he actually said hardly made an impression. One could not pin him down. Insensibly Alexis had come to confuse the manner of Socrates's speech with what he had been saying. And Socrates's manner, as the indignant jury agreed, had been intolerable. The shameless man had cracked jokes. He had likened the Democracy to a brave, but stupid horse. He had told them with a twinkle in his eye that Apollo's oracle had pronounced him the wisest man in Greece. He had not begged for mercy, as was the custom, or introduced his young children to do so for him. Blandly, obstinately, he maintained that he was extremely good for the state. Even his friends on the jury, though voting for acquittal, showed chagrin.

The jury condemned. The charge had been treated

as a perfectly frivolous affair, while its own authority had been almost openly laughed at. "Teach him to grin at us," muttered Dinon, wagging his beard. Alexis had to agree. So obvious, in fact, was the indignation of the jury that Anytos was emboldened to ask the penalty of death.

At this Alexis hesitated again, though the answer of Socrates added fuel to his wrath and did not provide him with an acceptable alternative. The outrageous old man was actually suggesting that he be given free meals, after the traditional fashion of rewarding those who had well served the state. Even his friends had started up at this and plucked him by the cloak. There had been a scene in court while the supporters of Socrates had clustered about him with protesting gestures. The water clock had dripped on, still measuring solemnly the time he had left to make a proper proposal. Finally Socrates had offered to pay a tiny fine, which at the insistence of his friends he had raised to a sum they could easily afford. Prison, exile, or any serious punishment would, he pointed out, deprive the state of his essential services in future. Once more, shamelessly, he smiled as he said this.

"Well!" Dinon muttered to his friend. "Did you ever hear the like of that?"

None of them ever had. There was nothing whatever the jury could do but make a mockery of its own verdict or sentence the obstinate old man to death. Alexis had not felt so angry since the news had come of the Spartan massacre of their prisoners after Aegospotami. In each case he had raged against the inevitable. At that time, the Spartans had cut Athens off from her food supplies and rendered her powerless. On this occasion, Alexis would have to vote for death to uphold the authority with which he had been entrusted.

"He'll escape," he said, trying to find consolation.

"To be sure he will," Dinon agreed. "D'you think the Eleven will keep close guard on the old fellow? Anyway, his rich friends will bribe them. What does it matter as long as the city is rid of him once and for all?"

"That's right." But Alexis wondered if any man but himself still thought of Pericles, who was so long ago dead. This Socrates had known him.

Socrates seemed glad to die. He said that death meant either eternal night or the company of the illustrious dead. He was happy with either alternative, though the city for its reputation's sake might have waited for nature to put an end to him. At his age, this would not have taken long. Presently the guards led him away, while the jury betook themselves to the places where they got their pay. Thence they scattered, still arguing, either homeward or to the modest taverns where houseless men like Alexis bought their dinner.

All was over, and yet not over. Everybody in Athens had a friend on the jury, or had heard Socrates talk, or had listened to the trial. The names of Critias and Alcibiades, the tyrannies of the Thirty, the loss of the war, the value of education — all were bandied about across the tavern tables with coarse wit, bitterness, or laughter. Few actually disputed the verdict because the friends of

Socrates were among the well-to-do. But the manner of Socrates's defense and the jury's dilemma gave rise to a great deal of mockery, all painful because it recalled things that Socrates had said. Out of their context and without the irritation of his demeanor, many sounded like echoes from the days of glory. "I thought that I ought not to do anything common or mean when in danger." Or: "The difficulty, my friends, is not to avoid death, but to avoid unrighteousness; for that runs faster than death." Or: "To discourse daily about virtue is the greatest good of man." Alexis could neither leave nor bear to listen. He lingered with his modest measure of watered wine, thinking dully that his own time was nearly come to find out what death was like. Stupidly he wondered why anyone troubled himself when an old man died, be it naturally or in some other way. Alexis did not know how to cope with his emotions. In fact, he hardly knew he had them. He had never concerned himself particularly with virtue before, never exhorted himself how to behave, never cared who perished when so many were dying — except for Pericles and his own sons. His tavern friends thought mistakenly that he was getting drunk, and they left him alone.

The talk went on and on. Given a good enough subject, there was no end to Athenian talk, no decent reticence, no word left unspoken. Proud of his memory, someone quoted with laughter, "If you kill such a one as I am, you will injure yourselves more than you injure me." Alexis stumbled abruptly to his feet and limped out.

The night air recalled him to his senses. He almost wondered if the wine could really have gone to his head. He had merely earned his dinner and had eaten it. Tomorrow, if he were lucky in the lot, he would do so again. Meanwhile, the time had gone by for getting a ride home. It would have been safer to go out earlier into the fields and sleep there, since even a poor old man wore cloak or sandals which might be considered worth stealing. In his strange mood, Alexis had not thought about the coming of dark.

He went stumbling down the pitch-black street, feeling his way with his staff, since often people threw heaps of rubbish out at times when the neighbors were not alert to protest. For a little while, he managed to follow an elderly citizen who was being lighted home. This, however, soon took him out of his way. He turned into the blackness again, having in mind a deserted corner of the Assembly Hill where he had previously spent a night under the stars. When he came out of the shadow of these narrow alleys, he would feel safer because . . .

Someone bumped into him savagely. Alexis, temporarily winded, gave a strangled gasp and fell, his bad leg twisted beneath him. He clutched at his cloak, but his assailant kicked, doubtless aiming for his head, but landing on his shoulder. Alexis groaned. His cloak was torn from his feeble grasp, and running footsteps pattered down the alley as the thief made off with his booty.

Alexis groaned and tried to get up. His clutching fingers groped on the ground about him for his staff. His knee was agony, and the night air already struck cool without a cloak. He could not hobble very far. Perhaps he could batter at some door, but dirty beggars half clothed and covered with dust were never welcome to folk already in bed. He began to thrust about with his staff to feel the walls between which he lay. It might be better to crawl up under one till pain subsided.

Prodded by his staff, a door creaked slightly ajar. No light came through it, but sounds were audible within. Somewhere in the recesses of this carelessly guarded house, a woman was scolding. Alexis could not hear what she said, but the shrewish tones were unmistakable, as was the length of her tirade. Nobody answered.

It took him a long time to get the door open and work

his way down a passage, partly sliding himself against the wall and partly hopping, aided by his trusty staff. All this time the woman went ranting on, speaking very fast and never apparently pausing once to catch her breath. The husband never answered a word, though accusations of neglect and self-indulgence poured over his head in a continuous wave. Presently Alexis found himself at the entrance to a small court; and looking across it to the open alcove on the other side, he saw a light.

There was not one man standing mute, but two. A slave beside them held a torch as though they had lately come in. There were stools in the alcove, but neither had used them. They watched the woman, who was striding up and down, now turning on them, now wheeling to gesture at a boy — or was it two boys who crouched in the shadow together?

"Never thought of his family once, never once in all these years . . ." the woman screamed, raising her hand to her black hair which she had already torn partly loose so that it straggled down her neck. She was a woman, as the torchlight cruelly showed, devoid of glamour. Strongly built and clumsy of movement, she was dressed in the plainest of heavy wool tunics girt up carelessly and of a dirty gray which suggested poverty or a complete disregard for her appearance. Far otherwise were the two brothers who watched her — the tall one and the broad one. Both were beautifully and meticulously dressed, while the slave they had with them wore a tunic of snowy white like the slave of a rich man.

Alexis took this in for a moment, still supporting himself against the wall, while he hesitated about how to interrupt. The woman was repeating herself again and again. "Never worked . . . Never earned us a penny . . . Lounging, talking, drinking with his fine friends. Coming home very late at night and off again early. See what he's brought us to now with all his talk of virtue. I told him . . . 'Mark my words,' I said . . . But he doesn't mind dying. Why should he? He's an old man now. We still have lives to live, but we never mattered. So he concerns himself to die with dignity while his poor children starve. We'll do better without him. Yes, better without him, I say. Let him throw his life away for all we care. Why should we think of him when he never thought of us once?"

She had come full circle again and was standing in the glare of the torchlight, her features working as she plucked at the disordered folds on her breasts.

One of the boys in the shadow made a movement, but before he could so much as stand up, the woman was on him. "Your father's destroyed himself, yes, he has. D'you think these fine friends of his will help us now? See them stand there and say nothing! Couldn't they have stopped him? Oh, oh! Why should he desert us?"

Alexis thrust out his staff and tried to take a step forward without the assistance of the wall. His leg, however, refused to support him at all. He only saved himself by falling back again with an agonized groan.

"Who's there?" In spite of the noise she was making,

the woman seemed all ears. She swiveled around and stopped speaking, so that a great silence seemed to fall. The servant raised the light of his torch to shine it on old Alexis, leaning against the farther wall, his eyes half closed, his face and tunic and beard all gray with dust.

"Get out of here, old man!"

"Get out at once. This is no place for strangers. Get out before we have the servant throw you." The two young men advanced on Alexis, seeming to find in him an object whereon to relieve their overcharged feelings.

"Old man, you had better be off. My mother's ill." The oldest boy — there were three of them after all — seemed about sixteen. He spoke with grave calmness, less excited by his mother's frantic mood than the two young men.

Alexis, whose good leg was giving way weakly, slid down against the wall and sat, sick and dizzy, not much caring whether he attracted pity or no, as long as nobody laid a hand on his bad leg.

"Get up!" The tall young man bent down to jerk at his arm. "Get up, I say!"

Alexis groaned.

"Don't be foolish, Adeimantos. The old man's hurt." It was the woman who thrust the others aside and bent over Alexis. "Shine the light on him. Ah, yes!" She dropped to her knees and ran a heavy, work-roughened hand down his leg so very gently that he did not even stir. "Hold him firm by the shoulders . . . so! Don't let him move." She seized his foot and gave it a great jerk. Alexis screamed. There was a click, and something fell into place. He felt an exquisite relief from agony and tried to gather his swimming senses. "That leg needs heat on it," the woman said, "to take away the pain." She lurched ungracefully to her feet. "I'll boil some water."

She was gone, her manner sober and completely practical, except for a shuddering sigh that she gave as she went. Hardly had her broad back disappeared into the women's rooms when the boy said in his grave, quiet way, "Sirs, I must thank you in my mother's name for being messengers from my father in his prison. Now she has recovered her senses, there is nothing that your kindness can do for us this night. Perhaps tomorrow she will be recovered enough to speak of the future."

Adeimantos hesitated, looking uneasily at the boy and at Alexis lying between them on the ground. There was a silence.

"Old man," said his broad-shouldered brother, leaning over Alexis, "we must not trouble the wife of Socrates on this night of sorrow. Can you get to your feet?"

He offered Alexis his arm, and the old man began to struggle to get his good leg under him again. The boy protested.

"My mother has a gift for healing, and it does her good to use it. Leave the old man with us."

Alexis was recovering his wits. He shook his head. "I'll not stay . . . help me out." He glanced around des-

perately, in a panic to be gone before the woman came
back with bandages and hot water. His staff was still on
the ground out of his reach.

"It is not fitting," Adeimantos said, but he spoke dubiously.

"I'll not stay here," cried Alexis, protesting more
loudly, "with the wife of Socrates. I was . . . I was on
the jury."

Even the square-shouldered one gave a gasp at that,
while the boy, who had been so calm and sensible, put
his hands before his face and burst into tears. The other
children, who had moved to stand behind him, began
wailing also.

"I have had Socrates's own couch moved into the
men's apartments." The woman came bustling back, her
manner brusque. "If Adeimantos or Plato will carry
him in, we need not detain them over our affairs any
longer. He must not yet walk."

"He . . . he is expected at home," Adeimantos stammered.

"Nonsense! Send your man to his home with a message."

"I shall go! I shall go!" cried Alexis even more wildly.

The boy lifted his tear-stained face from his hands and
said, "He was on the jury." He began to sob again in the
midst of a dead silence.

"What was the jury to do?" cried Alexis, beside himself. He turned on Plato, who still had him by the arm.

"Socrates insulted the court. By laughing at our justice, he defied the whole democracy. We had to condemn him."

Plato removed his arm. "Who were you to condemn such a man as he? What do you know about justice? What is your democracy but as great a tyranny as that of the Thirty? Why, even Critias, mad dog though he became, was an enemy worth having. This poor rustic fool takes a man's life and apologizes, saying, 'Socrates insulted the court.' If Socrates had not, you should have condemned him for pretending to virtue."

"Leave the poor old man alone," Adeimantos protested, his hand on his brother's shoulder. "Must I remind you that the nephews of Critias may never utter a word against democracy?"

"I'll say what I please tonight," Plato retorted. "I don't care. Democracy's dead, and Justice with her." He looked scornfully at Alexis. "Or very nearly dead, the pitiful old thing! I've done with both of them. You might as well tell Protos to hand us over his torch and carry this old democrat out. I like to imagine that if we left him here, Xanthippe might kill him."

"There was not anything else we could do, I tell you," Alexis protested.